Pot Likker, Pulley Bones, and Pea Vine Hay

Faye Brown
Illustrations by Trillie Brown

SEVGO PRESS • Northport, Alabama

FIRST PRINTING - OCTOBER 1987
SECOND PRINTING - FEBRUARY 1988
THIRD PRINTING - SEPTEMBER 1988
FOURTH PRINTING - JANUARY 1989

Library of Congress Cat. Card No. 88-61254
ISBN 0-943487-02-1

PRINTED IN THE UNITED STATES OF AMERICA
SEVGO PRESS, 1955 – 22nd STREET, NORTHPORT, AL 35476

To the memory of my father
Ira Porter
and to the honor of my mother
Pearlie Shirley Porter
whose hard work, faith, and laughter
pulled us through the tough end
of these Great Depression tales.

Contents

'Fore We Get Goin'. . .

Pot likker, pulley bones, and pea vine hay pulled Mama and Daddy and us nine younguns' through the Great Depression. Well, the pea vine hay actually pulled our short-teated cow, Ole Bossy, through the straights. And then her buttermilk made the cornbread to sop the pot likker to prolong our flesh upon the land. And the pulley bones — those we kids "pulled" after the preacher'd eaten the meat — well, getting the long end of the bone with it's promise of "better times" sustained my spirit through 20 lean years as an Alabama tenant farmer's child.

Pot likker, pulley bones, and pea vine hay pulled me back together after some "highlights" in my life: After a bathing with Granny Porter's lye soap, a "thrashing" with Mama's brushbroom, and Grandma Shirley's cold treatment (her mullen cough syrup and kerosene 'sear cloth').

The three P's snatched me from the wounds of the spurring roosters and the flogging setting hens; from the injuries I sustained while hanging onto the ground slide when my brother Bill let our old mule, Frank, run away, dumping and shredding enough cabbages to make kraut for a German army.

The pot likker renewed the vigor that was sapped from me while fighting Johnson grass, boll weevils, and stinging worms with my sisters Frances, Sue, Betty, and Trillie on the back forty. It compensated for the energy lost chasing my younger brothers Doug, Donald, and Shirley Ray—and doing it while sweltering under long-sleeved guano sack shirts and big bonnets (the head wear invented by someone bent on smothering children at an early age and thus exterminating the human race).

It looked like that death-defying ride on Bill's homemade truck wagon down a cliff side, with a 90-degree turn beside a giant oak; it seemed for sure that ride was gonna be my last, but I survived, with the help of pot likker and a pulley bone. These latter also revived my fainting heart the day Bill put the green snake down my bibbed overalls.

A dashing young man by the name of Joe Brown took me fishing and promised to help me overcome my dependency on the 3-Ps; I married him. Thirty years later I must confess: it was the juice from the cheap turnip greens—the pot likker—and the pulley-bone promises that kept us going at times. For instance, when, in the space of 24 hours, Joe's job fell through, our eldest, Greg, swerved to miss a "deer" and totaled a car against a tree, our precocious Glenda called from college and confessed she'd blown her tuition money on name-brand jeans, and our youngest, Glenn, set the entire county's forest ablaze.

And here I am, still depending on pot likker and pulley bones. Depending on them to strengthen me through my memory-loss and the arthritis known as "typewriter elbow". And if they will uphold me just a little longer I want to share with you my stories about *"Pot Likker, Pulley Bones, and Pea Vine Hay."*

New Mall Reminds Me Of The Rolling Store

I shopped at the new mall for the first time last week. I had heard it was a marvel of modern merchandising. So you can imagine my surprise to find it so similar to Mr. Eulie's rolling store where I bought stuff as a kid.

Double doors led into the Galleria and a friendly person stood just inside, welcoming me. It was the way Mr. Eulie'd done. He would always stop his little store-on-wheels on the side of the dirt road, swing wide the two wooden doors and say, "howdy, howdy." Then while he asked my brother and me about our folks and discussed the weather he'd commence figuring up the chickens Bill'd brought down in the tow sack and the eggs I'd toted in the little frazzled basket.

He counted, then put the eggs with others in a big wooden crate. With heads tucked underneath their wings, the hens lay very still while the scales balanced and Mr. Eulie totaled their worth on a *Big Red* tablet. The squawking birds were then put into a cage out back, right beside the drum. Bill was allowed to turn the crank on the latter while the kind old man filled our tin can with one gallon of kerosene and subtracted ten cents from our credit.

After Bill and I had climbed the two steps into the cavernous aisle we stood with wide eyes and open mouths, surveying the shelves-upon-shelves of beautiful, wondrous items from near and far. For whereas the modern establishment I visited days ago required one or more huge stores for the stocking of each item, Mr. Eulie had been able to craftily assemble all the same things into one tight space. With a magical glance you could see the tobacco products, the coffees and teas, the ready-made garments, the rare foods, the soda waters, the candy, and on and on. It was almost more than our young hearts were able to stand when Mama sent us the two miles to meet the rolling store once a week.

I noticed a lot of the clerks in the mall standing patiently like Mr. Eulie always did, just letting folks look and knowing they'd not be buying very much at all. Years ago we would look at the *Brown Mule Chewing Tobacco.* And all the snuff — the *Navy,* the *Tube Rose,* and the *Garrett Sweet Snuff* — knowing full well we wouldn't buy any unless Granny came to visit. We'd usually buy one sack of *Country Gentleman Tobacco* for Daddy but when there was enough money Mama'd send for his favorite, *Prince Albert Smoking Tobacco* in the flat red can.

We'd reverently touch the cans, bottles, and bags of many things—the sardines, the salmon, the tomatoes with pictures on the sides, the *Royal Cup* and the *Luzianne Coffee* with chicory, and—during the war years—the coffee substitute, *Postum.* We'd marvel at the stacks of vanilla flavoring, the black pepper, and the rice, which sometimes had weevils crawling around inside the bags.

The packaged corn meal was also a fascination to us since we always ground ours at the grist mill. During rainy weather we'd notice that the little five-pound cloth bags of salt were as hard as rocks. I'd imagine them as reproductions of Lot's wife leaving Sodom. And, on the shelf right above, looking down at them in shame, were the stern preachers wearing black hats on the *Quaker Oats* boxes.

Close at hand Mr. Eulie had folded the overalls, the khakis, and the socks. And there were the blue denim shirts for a dollar each. I saw the same line of goods, including straw hats for working in the fields and long johns for winter, in a mall store called The Banana Republic. My heart went out to that 'Banana fellow', not being able to sell his $32 denim shirts since the sun had, obviously, already faded them. And I knew he must be a struggling merchant since he'd used old rough lumber in his place like Mr. Eulie'd had to do.

Brightly flowered shorts were being sold right and left in the new conglomerate. The rolling store sold them also, in a roundabout way. Flour came in printed bags and after my Mama emptied the 25-pound sacks she changed them into bloomers for my sisters and me. Mr. Eulie sold printed dresses, too; as cloth on bolts, not ready-mades.

The swanky hotel that is part of the latest complex also contributed to my comparison with the rolling store. The pattern of the red-marbled bathroom floors looked like the old store's did on rainy days after Bill and I coated them with squishy red clay from our bare feet. And folks lounging on the soft sofas in the lush lobby seemed as relaxed as Mr. Eulie years ago when he plopped down on one of his old weathered apple crates.

Now even though the mall is all spread out in many directions I noticed most of the activity seemed to revolve around the middle of the place just like it did in the rolling store's center aisle. That was where Bill and I'd stand and pore over the stick candy for seven kids: "Should we get three red - and - whites and four yellow - and - whites, or should it be four red - and - whites and three yellow - and - whites?" And that was also where we stood licking our *BB Bats* when Mama'd allow us a few extra pennies.

As I lingered at center court, eating with hordes of others this past Easter, I spied the modern chicken coop and their egg crates. The chickens were already cooked and they called the coop the *Chick-Fil-A* place. The eggs were a dark brown, had been wrapped in plastic, and lay in small boxes in the window of a store called Godiva's.

I rationalized that perhaps the main center mall attraction was the bright elongated red lights high overhead. They seemed so familiar — like the lantern that Mr. Eulie hung from the ceiling of his rolling store on particularly dark, stormy days.

And the fountain at center court with its water flowing downhill in a steady stream reminded me of the time Mr. Eulie reached down and grabbed a gallon jug of white vinegar. Thinking he had gotten the water jug—the one he always took along for drinking and filling his truck's overheated radiator—the big swig he took into his mouth immediately came out again—in a stream very similar to the modern fountain in the mall.

Leaving the mall recently I noticed two final things that took me back across the years. The white bags in which folks carried their purchases had writing on the sides, proclaiming such things as Macy's, Sears, and J. C. Penney. The white guano sacks Bill and I usually swung across our shoulders with flour and sugar therein said things also, like 6-8-4 and 8-8-8.

Turning back for one last look I gasped to see a camel, kneeling near the doorway of a store. It looked the world like our old mule, Frank, the day we rode him to the rolling store to bring back coffee, salt and laying mash. Bill let the old mule's foot slip through the bridge and down he fell, on both front knees, the way that camel did outside the mall's new fancy place. And the sacks resting on Frank's back looked for the world like the camel's hump.

Since I spent ten hours in that "ultimate Shopper's Paradise" I've had a lot of time to compare the place with Mr. Eulie's rolling store, of conditions now and decades past. I've thought on "hurting tootsies" and business; I've come up with an idea I feel would be good for both in years to come. Put down a red dirt road for flooring and change the shoe code to *nothing but bare feet.*

They Oughta Swap Their Feed Sacks

I was embarrassed for the sitcom couple when the cameras showed it. It happened when the TV caught their kitchen as millions like me gaped in amazement. The apple crates nailed on our wall years ago exposed things to the world also. And, just like the boxes we put up, theirs held their dishes—their jelly glasses, their chipped plates and their little crystal dish premiums from the oatmeal boxes.

The cameras didn't zoom in close enough for me to tell if the medicine bottles were *Cardui* or *Syrup of Black Draught* but the short box was definitely *Carter's Little Liver Pills.* I figure after humiliation like that the wife arose at dawn to dye the guano sacks and cover the kitchen crates with curtains like Mama did ours years ago.

I recently experienced sorrow touring a newly acquired old house. As the owner proudly pointed to the 14-foot ceilings I thought of the trouble I have getting cobwebs from my 8-foot ones. I tried to imagine what a bad place she musta' just moved from—since she excitedly showed off all the old chifforobes, and I noticed that was all she had for storage space. I figured the latch on the one in the den wasn't working because the doors were ajar, exposing her old quilts to the world. I went home and prayed that someday that lady'd be able to know the joy of hiding things behind closet doors and of having a dual-controlled electric blanket like I do.

Fact is, I've noticed a lot of folks lately are having to swing back to the olden days. My sister just got a new house, but they weren't able to afford all the extras. I slept over the other night and fumbled in the dark five minutes before realizing they'd sacrificed wall switches. Betty answered my "arms thrashing in mid-air distress" by locating a dangling string to illume the room and start a fan to humming, just like we did four decades ago when the Pow'r Com'ny first gave us lights.

I overheard a young mother having conniptions in Wal-Mart. She was thrilled senseless over having located the new-fangled fold or twist curlers for her daughter's hair. They were nothing more than strips cut from a *Prince Albert* tobacco can covered with plastic instead of the brown paper sack we always used.

And in the mall I saw a mad rush on ankle-boots printed like a newspaper, looking for the world like those Dad and the nearby men fixed up during the monstrous snows of the lean 30's. They had achieved the look by wrapping and tying papers around their holey shoes as insulation and protection against frostbite.

There's been a real reversal, also, back to boldly showing brand names on one's clothing. Today the labels proudly announce *Lee, Levi, Reebok, Nike,* or *Calvin Klein.* Long ago ours said *Martha White Self-Rising* or *Purina Checker-Board Square.*

I can recall during real hard times, when we kids shot up a mile in one year, that sometimes Mama'd be forced to lengthen our dresses with ruffles of a different pattern. And there were a few mornings, when my sister wouldn't let me borrow her solid sweater or I couldn't sneak out of the house without one, that Mama made me wear my printed one over my plaid skirt. But that was unusual — everyone went to great lengths back then to coordinate their clothing.

We saved the pretty fabric sacks (from the laying mash we had to buy for the hens in the dead of winter). And we walked miles and miles—to Mrs. Mamie's, and Mrs. Clara's, and Mrs. Nettie's — back and forth, swapping feed sacks 'til we had enough to make a matching dress.

I feel like the total breakdown in today's

fashions just reflects our lack of neighborly love. Recently I've seen young girls everywhere — schools, church, TV — all having to combine printed skirts, checked blouses, and geometric jackets. And often they're so short on fabric their dresses incorporate all three designs. It just breaks my heart; I keep wishing they had a good neighbor nearby to whom they could go and swap their feed sacks.

The FDA Would've Nailed Grandma To The Wall Over Her Winter Cold Remedies

Early on in fall, with the realization my family was headed full-speed into the flu season, I laid in a big supply of *Contac*, *Dristan*, and *Puffs*. (It was the least I could do for the good sponsors on TV).

Being warned by an accountant that this was my final chance to get a tax break on insulation (and fend my family from the cold as well), I laid another 18 inches in the attic, affixed a second set of storm windows outside the first, and chinked the last air hole with five layers of polyurethane.

I lay back on the couch, pleased with our readiness for winter. Then Dr. Dean Do-Tell came on the evening news. First, he gave a warning against the use of antihistamines. Then he reported that these airtight homes invite health cares with no end. They cause the indoor humidity to drop, dry out nasal membranes, and bring on everything from colds to the dreaded long-face syndrome. A letter from my dentist confirmed his very words.

But yet and still — with the flu outbreak already in Alaska and quickly heading south — I couldn't just sit idly by. Not with the possibility of my loved ones being hit early in the new year with either the *Philippine-A*, the *Chilean-A*, or the *Russian-B*, or worse yet, the chance that all three of these might get together and mutate (or whatever) into an entirely different strain.

I knew the possibility at this late date of getting a vaccine for a new flu type, say a *Beirut-Z*, would be nil. You see, these target viruses have to be grown in chicken eggs. And having lived on the farm, I know full well that near Christmas the hens are on such a strike that you have to use gourds for nest eggs just to keep them reminded of the shape.

So what kind of medication should we use for winter ills? In an effort to solve my problem I decided to confer with Mom. She said the homemade cough syrup handed down by grandma would be easy for me to make. First I had to boil together three plants: sweetgum buds, mullen, and the tender ends off pine trees. Honey and alum must then be added to the strained liquid before it was bottled for use on the first (unsuspecting victim) to fall ill.

Grandma had advocated the use of a poultice made with crushed mustard seed for a bad chest congestion. Mama had devised her own variation: camphor, turpentine and kerosene mixed together on a piece of wool or flannel. Before this "sear cloth" was pinned to undergarments a coating of tallow was applied to prevent blistering of the skin. (I recall vividly that wearing such a cloth had the same effect on my friendships as the Biblical lepers' cry of "UNCLEAN! UNCLEAN! UNCLEAN!" had on theirs).

After forever marrying MY image with the likes of the above, my Mama then had the audacity to try it on my youngest son as well. While I was away teaching one day she bundled the sickly child and summoned my sister to take him to the pediatrician. Both Sis and Doctor Reese (the angel in a medic's coat) were shocked to discover the source of his weird smell: a Vick's Salve saturated cloth my Mom had placed between chest and shirt of the small lad.

My Mama's only comment about the incident was that the one who'd brought me into this world, a kindly Dr. Shackleford, had recommended *Vick's* or *Mentholatum* on a rag, to "open up bronchitis in the chest." For the very tiniest of her babes she'd substituted camphorated oil instead.

I didn't need to be reminded of grandma's earache remedies. Her boiled peach seed liquor had been put into my ear. And I used her other one so much as a child it's now hard to sleep without the smell of toasty-hot cornmeal, tied in a cloth, next to my head.

There's one thing that Mama never quibbles over, however, when talking modern medicine with me. My sister Trillie's bout with whooping cough made strong supporters of her and Dad when the vaccine DID come out. As the child leaped from bed, night after night, without warning, and raced — it was my Dad's quick pursuit and firm grasp that always plucked her — just as she flung her gasping, whooping self to porch's edge. (If only they had listened to grandma and put asafetida on a string about her neck).

My husband and son are already experiencing breathing problems. (Do you think from the 148 uninterrupted hours of deer hunting in the rain and cold? NAW. More likely from the desert-like conditions in this air-tight house). And any day now one of them may come down with a bad case of some type flu. Being a concerned wife and mother I'm caught between a rock and a hard place over possible medications to be used.

Shall I risk the bad effects of modern medicines? Or pit myself against the wrath of the Food and Drug Administration in its current crackdown against medical quackery? Whatever route I choose for now one thing looms crystal clear: If the FDA had've been active a few years back they would've sure nailed Grandma's and Mama's hides to the wall!

Stuck With Molasses And Perfumed Table Salt

My daughter now bubbles about the deep, enchanting snows she's enjoying in Massachusetts, New Hampshire, and Vermont. I reacted that way to lots of snow a few times in my youth as well. Once was in the Alps of Bavaria three decades back; the most memorable was in Alabama many years ago.

The winter, from the grown-up point of view, had already been a long, lean one for us. The only bright spots had been Christmas and the birth of another child, the fifth, just after the dawning of 1940. Elated, as always, over the coming of another baby, Daddy felt the beautiful little girl meant better times.

Keeping the house warm enough for a newborn had taken its toll on the firewood. As Daddy daily piled huge backsticks, along with smaller logs and rich pine splinters into the fireplace, he eyed with anxiety the dwindling woodpile.

Mama completed her decreed two weeks in

bed following childbirth and took a little walk outside the door late one afternoon. She announced that she could again manage the house without her husband's gentle help.

So Daddy took up a bottle, filled it with kerosene, and stuck green pine needles in the top. He made sure the crosscut saw was sharp; he and the neighbor would replenish our woodpile next day.

But then it came—with silence and stealth that very night, the way a robber comes. And well might history call it 'The Thief' instead of simply 'The Big Snow' — the way it wrested peace of mind from rich and poor adults alike.

Very few in this deep South state were ready for a two-foot snow. It took a carefree seven-year-old like myself to scrape the makings of a snowball off the bedcovers in happy glee. I couldn't figure Mama's worry over cracks within the shack, or Dad's despair about the brilliant beauty piled outside.

Snow dipped from near the kitchen door and melted in containers upon the cooking stove supplied our water for some days. When Daddy finally scooped the snow to either side and made a path up to the neighbor's yard, I begged to help bring drinking water from the well; (a chore I usually frowned upon).

Going up and down the hill became a greater thrill after water spilled to form a solid sheet of ice within the high snow walls. I scooted daringly along on thin-soled shoes when Mama'd let me out of sight. I became the boy my teacher'd read about, *Hans Brinker of the Silver Skates*. Or Napoleon's daring soldier behind the snowy banks of Russian hills of whom I'd heard at Mama's knee.

Mostly my sister, Frances, and I kept busy in the house. The pages from the catalog that weren't folded inside Daddy's holey shoes became our paper dolls, with many clothes for every one. We sewed quilt squares and played continuous games of jacks.

While Mama and the small ones took a nap we churned the butter near the hearth. When toddler Sue arose we made her play off in the kitchen, safe from the fire, so Mom could get her rest. We pointed out the many buckets of the sorgham syrup from Grandpa over in the corner of the room. At first it was the shiny pails that kept her there. But after one turned over it was the sweet and sticky molasses that held her captive in more ways than one. After Mom awoke and found her thus it was a time before my older sis and I were caught up so within our books.

We girls were jealous of our ten-year-old brother, Bill, who trudged in hip-high snow wherever Daddy went. They gave the mules a lot of fodder and corn shucks down at the barn, they milked the cow inside the stall, and soon they sawed the wood out in the bitter cold. Or so Daddy said it was; Bill took it all within his stride.

When the snow had melted down enough to

let the wagon axle clear the top they made the four-mile trip to check on Granny and to borrow salt. Unthinking, Granny poured the salt from a five pound sack into a small box just emptied of its perfumed starch from Blair. For the next three weeks Mama had a clear-cut choice: serve unsalted food or food that had a slight perfume.

With pining hearts we children bade a sad goodbye to "The Big Snow" near Saint Valentine's own day. But to Mom nor Dad nor other grown folks 'round about we dared not voice our hurt at seeing once again the earth all common brown; they claimed it was a view from heaven sent to them.

But during all the snowed-in weeks my folks acquired some strong convictions of their own. To the day of Daddy's death he never let his woodpile get so low nor his syrup buckets stacked so high. He viewed with great disdain any gathering of snow clouds.

And 'til this very hour my Mama stocks up on salt as soon as colored leaves begin to fall. She has not yet a strong desire for sweet fragrances within her kitchen walls. She doesn't skip one chance to leave the house on winter days—lest snow should fall and close her in again for six long weeks. Mom's never got excited over modern weather men who mention heavy snowfalls' likelihood. And now I find that even I have reached the age to join with her in thinking big snows are mostly for the young.

I Fibbed About Milking Ole Bossy

I hate to admit it to Mama and my brother Bill but years ago I did fib about milking our new cow, Ole Bossy. I crossed my fingers behind my back when I told them it was impossible for me to get even a few drops out of her little short teats. (It seemed such a waste of time for me to spend thirty minutes pulling and squeezing to get milk that Bill could get in five).

I knew how it'd been with our other cows; Bill could let the little bull take a few sucks (so the stubborn mama'd let her milk down), yank the calf out of there, wash up the cow's bag, and the rest was a snap. If I let a young steer in to it's mama, the milk was history; I could never get him away till the last drop was gone.

Being a fast milker permitted Bill to head back to the house with the foam trickling over the bucket's rim long before a cow finished her fodder and shucks. When I milked? They ate all their food, grew restless, and sauntered away—leaving me and the near-empty pail sitting awkwardly in the midst of space.

Bill has ESP: he knew just when to dodge the cow's tail. But the horse flies got away when I was there and my face took the full brunt of the stiff hairs matted with "cuckle" burrs. And my big brother sensed when to jerk the bucket from between his squatted legs and jump. Not me—the cow's dirty foot would always land in my bucket of milk and I'd lay sprawled backwards, knocked off my little stool. I once grew so tired of it, I was thrilled to see Daddy "squash" that big toadfrog with the wagon wheel—I felt for sure our cow'd go dry soon.

Another thing that made Bill more suited for milking was his high-topped brogans. They were much better than my oxfords for wading in the "nice, soft hay" out at the barnlot when it'd been raining for a month of Sundays.

When "Old Sal" died and we got the new short-teated Bossy, neither was it a question of me thinking Mama ought to go back to milking on the cold winter mornings. She'd had her turn and deserved our help. When she'd had only babies and Daddy'd headed to the sawmill 'fore day, she'd been forced to leave us toddlers on a pallet—in the one room that wasn't freezing—while she went to the barn. With one end of a feedsack sheet tied about the bedpost and the other about our little waists, she'd prayed we wouldn't reach the open fire while she milked the cow, put out the calf, and threw down a few nubbins for the old mule.

No, Mama definitely shouldn't be the one to milk Bossy. I could remember her hectic mornings after we first babies had been rooted from her lap by more. With gentle but firm warnings about the little ones and fire, Mama had hurried to do the milking before we left for school. Leaving the baby-tending to my sister Frances, I'd stand near the frosted window and watch Mama rushing through the outside chores. The thin unlined coat, some gentleman's church garment three lives ago, now let it's wide lapel be lapped, then pinned, to warm my Mama's chest. The headrag, named "Mother's Best, 25 lbs.," long frayed by freezing, angry winds, huddled in a knot below her chin.

The milk and Mama'd both be puffing out steam like urgent smoke signals by the time I lifted the wooden latch and they hurried into the kitchen's warmth. "Run, I hear the bus a pullin' out from the Fairs' right now," Mama'd call. Then quickly placing the bucket on the cabinet she'd follow us through the house, "Button that coat, Frances. Did you get your spelling paper, Nonie Faye? You're forgetting your lunch, Bill."

—Yeah. By the time Bill and I reached

twelve and fourteen, Mama was definitely overdue for some help with the milking on cold mornings. So, looking back now—it seems hard to figure why I fibbed about my fingers being "too weak to get milk from Ole Bossy." It certainly wasn't that I didn't like milk. Well, I did hate the taste of the buttermilk, but it was needed for baking delicious cornbread to eat with good sweet milk every night. I remember with remorse the time we had no milk for supper and the fault lay with Bill and me.

If we had just done our work before our play. Now it usually took us less than a minute to do our before-dark chore of separating the calf from the cow: Bill'd grab the calf about the neck with his strong arms and half-push, half-ride him out of the gate. If the animal dared falter, Bill'd give his tail a quick, crisp twist and that'd be the end of his hesitation. The little switch I always carried never had a chance to sway the calf's actions, either way.

But that one particular spring night Bill and I chased lightning bugs till dark and forgot to take the calf from its mama. And the next morning there was not a drop of milk to be had. And for supper that night there was not a drop of milk to drink with our good cornbread. The water we drank with our meal was punishment enough to keep Bill and me remembering our chores for a long time afterwards.

Yes, milk was an important thing at our house. Why—I can remember it even being used as an instrument for the teaching of manners. The night I mistakenly gulped from a tall glass of buttermilk placed for my visiting Granny—and then immediately spit the sour liquid all over the table and the ten people around it—that night afforded Mama an opportunity to take me into the back room and impress upon me Emily Post's (or her own?) rules about "spitting milk at the table."

And before I forget my manners again—if you will excuse me, please—I'm going for a tall glass of good, cold milk. I'm working up the courage to admit to Bill and Mama that I was just lazy when I fibbed about not being able to milk Ole Bossy.

Hog's Head Cheese And Bladderballs

Hog-killing time had been decreed the afternoon before. It happened as Daddy studied the sky, felt the air, and determined that the clear, cold spell was "gonna hang on."

Early on the 'perfect day' my brother Bill'd gulp down his breakfast, hook the old mule to the ground slide, and go down the road a piece to our neighbor's.

By that time I had usually convinced Mama that I wouldn't miss much in school that day. It wasn't that I liked the butchering of the animal; in fact, I hated most of it. But there was just something about the good - natured hustle - and -

bustle on hog-killing day that made me say I'd stay and tend the babies.

Shortly, Bill'd be back, a steel drum and a washpot on the rough wooden vehicle. Mr. Homer, walking by his side, said Mrs. Mamie'd "be up as soon as the kids caught the bus."

From the kitchen window I'd see the men in their thin coats, shivering against the cold wind. They'd walk to the fires, rub their rough hands together, then spread them near the red flame tongues that licked the black pots' sides.

As Daddy came for the gun I ran to the farthermost room and stopped my ears against all sound. For although I hated the slopping of the hogs (and was glad to hear the preacher say the Prodigal Son came to his senses, quit feeding the swine, and went home to his rich Papa)—in spite of all this—I pitied the pigs, especially Ben.

From the time Ben was a piglet he'd lift his eyes higher from the ground than others in his litter. And even though he'd make me mad by dropping ears of bright yellow corn down in the mud, he stole my heart. I'd see him watch the red calf scamper in the wide, clean pasture over toward the hills. And in my heart I felt he wanted to be out and free—like the yearling.

The dead hog was scalded in the boiling water which filled the tilted, half-buried drum. Next it was placed on the nearby plank - and - sawhorse table. There the coarse hair was removed from the animal's skin by quick, hard scraping with sharp blades.

The women, hidden under coats, big aprons, and head rags, came out to assist and make sure the hog got a real smooth shave. That finished, the men attached a single-tree (from the mule's harness) to the tough tendons of the hog's legs. By that they swung him up to the strongest limb of the big oak, the one on which we put our tire swing in the summer.

The No. 3 washtub caught the hog's insides as Daddy made careful slashes with his razor sharp knife. The tub was then passed to the women.

The detached lights (lungs), liver, heart and kidneys were washed and taken into the house. Mama'd fry up some of the liver and serve it with gravy and hot biscuits for lunch in a little while. The other would be used, along with the cleaned hog's head and feet, to make hog's head cheese or souse.

The women pulled the fat from around the intestines (they worked very cautiously, fearful they'd make the slightest tear). After lunch they'd "cook it out" in the scrubbed-clean pots. They'd watch it like a "hawk watchin' chickens," lest it'd scorch and ruin our lard for the year.

The men placed the washed, beheaded carcass on the table and cut it up. From it they made hams, shoulders, sides of bacon, spareribs and backbones. Most of these would be cooled in the smokehouse overnight. They would then be salted down, and eventually scraped and hung over a hickory fire to smoke.

Unlike most of our neighbors, we didn't go for pickled pig's feet nor eating chitlins from the hog. Well, my baby sister says Mama did fry up some chitlins once. For years Trillie thought the horrible odor in the house that night was directly traceable to Bill's sleep-over friend.

With everyone now worn out they'd set aside the souse and sausage making until the following morning. Daddy'd give our neighbors a mess of meat to take back home. (They'd leave in time to "mosey on down, chunk up the fire, and throw on a good backstick so the kids won't have to come into a cold house").

When Bill took the entrails off on the slide he'd stop by the branch for a small reed. He'd later insert this into the rinsed hog bladder to inflate it. The bladderball, once dried, gave us many days of fun.

Now some folks save the best 'til last; not us. We ate high on the hog that very night. First Mama scrambled the brains with eggs. Then she fried some tenderloin and made gravy in the pan. Hot biscuits topped the feast that was enough to hold us until the following night when second-best always came around. The cornbread made with cracklin's, left over from the rendering of the lard, was always near the top for us when Daddy killed a hog.

When Popcorn Burned The Churnrag And Left Ashes On The Whey

Today's parents provide their children with winter night fun by bringing in video players and the latest tapes. Ours brought in a tub of shucked corn and set it in front of the fire. After supper we would each get a wobbly straight chair and gather round, vying for the best spot — the in-between place where you neither froze to death nor burned your legs from the blazing wood and the tub's hot rim.

First, Daddy'd row the ears—he'd shell off two or three columns of the grains—so little hands could more easily empty down the fuzzy cob. Then he'd start telling one of his haint-and-booger tales. These would get our minds off the tearing at our flesh by the sharp, resisting kernels of the corn.

Long before bedtime Mama'd switch us over to less unnerving things like rhymes about "Simple Simon" who met a pieman, or riddles asking, "How many were going to Saint Ives?" She didn't want us sleeping off across the hall with seven quilts pulled atop our heads, a shield against the scary creatures Daddy told about.

When the corn was shelled, and the cobs reduced to ashes, and the tub moved off into the corner, we'd inch our semi-circle closer to the dying fire and play, "Thimble, thimble, who's got the thimble?" or "Rock School" with some old button from the jar.

After Daddy chunked up the fire—pulled the burned sticks into the center, pushed the poker back and forth to send the little stars dancing up the chimney, and threw on another dry backstick—after Daddy'd done this we'd become quite warm and venture to the room's far reaches. There we would play jacks, dominoes or paper dolls. Or the boys would whittle down a slingshot stock.

Some long cold evenings we just sat, our heads in books like burrowed moles, and quietly enjoyed the pleasure of each other's company. It was then our elders read the Bible or turned down corners of the new seed catalogue.

Nothing helped block out the howling of the winter winds like cooking snacks out in the kitchen after supper. But before we could make the peanut brittle we had to shell the peanuts we had picked off the vines.

One of our favorite things was making molasses candy that had to be cooked, then pulled, and pulled, and twisted. While we did this we begged Mama to tell us, just one more time, about the Taffy Pulls with her 'fellers', when she was a young, pretty lass.

The highlight of the candy making was the way the dark redhead, the bubbling syrup, changed quickly into an auburn blonde when Mama dropped a pinch of soda in the pan. My second favorite thing about it was the time when we, with lard-protected hands, could take a lump of the bleached, hot candy and pull it back and forth and turn it into something grand—the way a player pulls an old accordion back and forth and brings out feasting for the soul.

Perhaps the thing we did most often on childhood winter nights was pop the corn that we had grown in fields during heated summer months. We popped it for eating plain, with salt or melted butter from the cow. And we popped it for making popcorn balls using the molasses Grandpa had cooked down at the syrup mill. But before the popping came the shelling by the fire. Sue and I always *just pretended* to do a good job of gathering the scattered grains and tossing them outside to be pecked next day by shivering, wind-tossed hens.

Our sins eventually found us out; they were revealed one night at bedtime when Mama got the sagebrush broom and began to "sweep up just a little." The vagabond grains were brought from their hiding places behind the bed frame's legs and from the rough floor's cracks. They were swept along with the dirt into the gray ashes at the hearth's warm edge. For just a little while they lay there, quietly, in the room's dim light. They began to smolder, then to blaze. Then suddenly the room became a tinderbox, a front-line war. The tiny fiery cannons exploded and flew, like dangerous shrapnel at every angle. They landed on Mama's neatly-tied churn rag, on the socks in Daddy's brogans by the wall, and on the feather pillows of the bed.

We jumped and yelled and fought with quilts and coats until the fires were all out. Only the clabbered milk was declared a total loss—the blazing flour sack had dumped its ashes and turned the cream to whey.

(Then came the time of reckoning for Sue and me—for failure to do well our job of taking dirty grains into the yard). As now in later years I'm looking back, I realize that all-in-all the fun we had and the things we learned around our fireplace long ago became the basis for the things worthwhile in our lives. It makes me wonder if the children who now must get their winter night fun from video cassettes will get their basic values from the tapes as well.

I Liketa' Been A Groundhog

I just missed it by an inch. Sometimes I almost blame Daddy. If he hadn't fooled around getting the fireplace finished I mighta made it. And if Mama hadn't been so set on 'borning me' in a particular place I mighta come a day sooner. As it turned out, I was born on the day they hurriedly moved into the little new house. It made me one day late for a nationally known birthday — Groundhog Day.

I've always felt that coming on February 2nd could've been my key to fame. Especially the to-do they make nowadays over important birthdays—everybody getting off work, folks making speeches, having parades, and even movie stars and the President sending cards and flowers.

This would have transpired, I suppose, if I'd

just arrived a few hours earlier: they would have called me Groundhog, in place of Faye. Well, when I was real little they mighta said Earth Pig instead. And they wouldn't have objected to my constant mud - pie - making nearly as much. And the best part of all — every year I could've slept straight through the cold January days.

And then on February 2nd I could've crawled out from the warm covers into the bright light of the TV cameras—with the whole nation watching, falling at my feet, praying I'd bring them not gloom, but sunshine for the next six weeks.

Although I missed out on such wide acclaim I've had at least two memorable birthday celebrations. Both came on bitter cold days when a "no-shadow woodchuck" would've been a blessed sight.

The first landmark party came when I was five. As my older siblings walked to the school bus they took a message to my next-door cousin; she was invited to walk down for lunch.

Mama interrupted our paper-doll-playing by the fireplace to serve the birthday meal. With Louise there, even the tomato soup and corn bread was special. But the surprise made our day.

Mama beat up an Everyday Cake, as she called it, and cooked part of it for the family's supper. Then, in odd-shaped tin cans hoarded for that very purpose, she baked two tiny cakes. Lacking modern day confectioners' sugar and birthday candles, she then garnished the golden-domed silos with dishes of blackberries, fresh-dipped from a Mason jar with memories of hot days and chiggers.

Sweet Sixteen is the other birthday stamped vividly in my memory book. The groundhog not only saw his shadow but sent the mercury plunging to a record minus three on the eve of my grandest party. My friend Jewel stayed overnight to help me clean and plan for the big Saturday night event.

Unmindful of Mama's warning, we decided to take advantage of the sleeping family to clean the kitchen floor. It didn't work—not with the burned-low fires and the frigid house. We spent several hours on our hands and knees, rubbing frantically with old towels and quilts, trying to dry the flour and remove the sheet of ice that had formed instantly when we spread the mop water on the rough pine boards.

Disregarding the steadily falling snow next day we continued our party preparations—we fried six dozen doughnuts from Mama's great recipe. We opened all her juice and readied three gallons of hot apple cider.

But our Post Office plans were doomed. Only one lone figure, crushing corn stalks beneath the snow, picked his way across the frozen field that night. Taking what comfort I could from a good friend by my side and a hot flat-iron at my feet, I finally drifted off to sleep feeling of a certainty things'd been better if I'd just been born a groundhog.

Valentine Box Magic

The Valentine boxes at school seemed to be filled with magic every year. But I had a feeling my fifth grade one was going to be something to remember; maybe it was because World War II had ended and the entire nation was in the mood for celebrating.

Right after Christmas the sale catalog with its pages and pages of Valentines arrived from Sears and Roebuck. My siblings and I spent hours dreaming about the large heart-shaped cards costing a nickel each. The penny ones, with the suckers attached, caused us to read over and over 'til we had memorized the descriptive words underneath. Our eventual choice had to lie, however, with the variety packs which were going that year for 29 cents per hundred.

Real diplomacy on Mama's part was required to negotiate a peaceful division when the Valentines arrived. There were enough 'Teacher' cards to go around, but only a few 'Special' ones. When my older brother and sister insisted on the largest cards with the mushy lines I didn't have the nerve to say I'd like one for a boy also. I just waited for the small ones to be divided out on an "eeney, meeney, mineey, moe" basis.

When the number of cards and classmates were counted I was short by one. I got the white tissue paper (that had come tucked in the toes of daddy's last pair of brogans) from its hiding place. A heated flat iron was used to make it smooth. Then Mama helped my faltering hands and mind remember the art of folding and cutting lacy hearts, which had been taught me earlier by Grandma.

When the fairy-like doily was glued to the flaming red heart (made from the construction paper that I had found in the trash can at school) — it was the most beautiful card in the house. I decided immediately it would be for my Secret One.

Mama didn't mind that I had raised my hand and volunteered cookies for the party. She didn't even mention that it meant that the family'd have no butter on their bread nor sweets for a week. Instead she lovingly assisted while I painstakingly cut around the waxed paper pattern to make 35 teacake hearts.

Perhaps—on the morning of the big day—my mind was too intent on concealing the frilly card I'd marked, "To: Ned — Be Mine, Love, Nona Faye." But when I realized, after boarding the school bus, that I'd left the bag of cookies behind, the day suddenly turned dark. I began to weep.

The kindly bus driver, Houston, returned the magic, briefly, to my day. He let my brother off to "run back for the cookies while the bus makes its five-mile loop." When Bill failed to arrive at the agreed connection in time, the driver doubled back for him. In the process the bus slid off the rain-slickened dirt road and into a ditch. I arrived in class two hours late, with puffed red eyes and the threat of my embarrassed brother hanging heavy over me.

Miss Hester had wrought a miracle transforming the square brown box into a huge white heart. The small red valentines glued randomly upon it completed the mirage. Gazing at it near the front of the room my thoughts raced wildly as the day's magic threatened again to alight upon me.

The glitter was short-lived. I was called aside and sent for the dreaded long walk to the principal's office. It seemed that the notes my friend Gracie and I had exchanged the day before had fallen into the administrator's hands. Gracie's secret love for Dean and mine for Ned were no longer a secret. My disgrace was compounded a thousandfold because the principal was also Ned's dad; his brief reprimand might well have been a cat-of-nine-tails.

I re-entered the classroom, sniffing, just in time to see Ned stuffing his cards into the beautiful box. What if his Dad had told and the huge red heart I now spied was marked for another?

Time for the party finally came. Gracie laid one white napkin on each cleared desk top. Earnestine gave every one a piece of candy and Meg distributed the sweets that she had baked. I felt really proud placing my pretty cookies all around; I even felt heady when Ned murmured, "MMMmmmmmmmm" as I moved slowly, awkwardly past him.

Miss Hester began reading aloud the names as helpers walked among us, delivering the precious cards. The stack on my desk grew larger and larger. Scanning the signatures of my many friends was no consolation now. Neither was the lollipop card from Sam (declaring that I was as sweet as the candy itself).

Meanwhile the pile in the large box dwindled smaller and smaller as my heart pounded harder and harder. Then I heard the name "NED" called. I turned just in time to see the smile he tried to hide upon viewing my filmy love token. Again I felt shame over yesterday's note to Gracie. Dared I have any hope?

As the last two cards came from the box the teacher called my name and extended a white envelope. Realizing the big red heart was not for me caused a ready tear to depart my eye—just before I saw, with great relief, Miss Hester place the lovely red card onto her own large heap.

Anxiously I tore open the envelope; a beautiful card peered out at me. There over a background of royal blue velvet shone a covering of lacy silver hearts, similar to my own art work. Turning it over, guardedly, I read the awkward scrawl — "Dad told me about the note. I'm glad. Will you be mine? Love, Ned." My blushing face turned ever so slightly to catch and return the twinkle in his eye and the smile on his lips. The Valentine Box really had held magic!

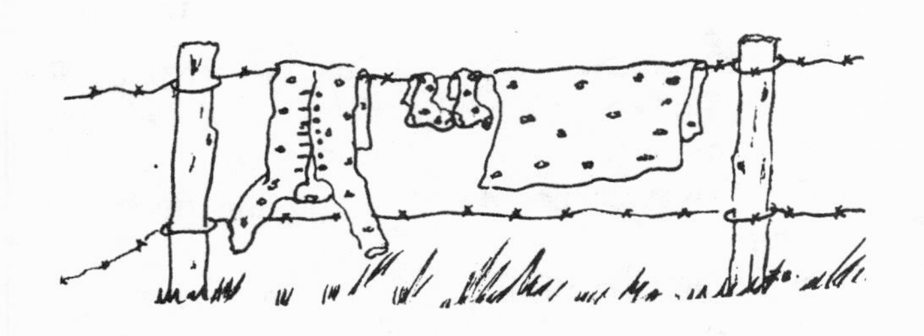

As Strong As Granny's Lye Soap?

To wager that something was "as strong as Granny's lye soap" was laying your life on the line. Many women, my Mama included, could make soap that'd cut lard from the kitchen floor, cold grease off the dishes, and a week's grime out of overalls — but they didn't dare hold their homemade soap up to Granny's.

During WW II when the country diverted its grease for explosives and during bad crop years when a bar of *Octagon* was beyond our reach, Mama made our soap using cans of *Red Devil Lye.*

Although the process didn't require boiling, Mama'd make the strong concoction in the yard, using a little iron pot. She'd put in about ten cups of water, then pour in two cans of the *Red Devil Lye.* While she dissolved the latter by stirring with a long stick, we didn't have to be told but once to keep our distance. The little red devil with the forked tail that danced on the can's label with his pitchfork aimed—ready to take us to Hell for disobeying like the preacher'd said he would—that devil was all the reminder we needed to stand WAY BACK while Mama stirred the dangerous mixture.

Sometimes Bill'd get a peep over the pot's rim when he handed Mama the bucket with the rank meat grease and the burned lard. From his privileged angle he'd holler, "WOW, just like magic th' way th' lye eats up th' grease. Look't it change color!" And sure enough, after Mama'd stirred about twenty minutes, the ten to twelve pounds of grease'd be gone and she'd dip the mushy substance into a shallow pan where we could all see its smooth, whitish texture.

Washing dishes with the soap after it'd been cut into neat little blocks wasn't too bad. In fact, it didn't seem to hurt my hands any more than the *Super Suds* my rich Aunt Margaret used in her dishpan. But when I rubbed clothes all day at the spring, I knew for sure the homemade soap wasn't as mild as the little bar of *Swan* we hoarded for hands and faces.

But washing with Mama's bar-soap was nothing compared to using the slimy-brown soap that Granny made. I was first introduced to it when she sent some in a little crock after my baby sister, Trillie, was born. My Aunt Zula—who'd come to care for Mama—and I began to be suspicious when Daddy said he hated to bring the soap into the house. He could remember having bathed in a washtub as a kid, using his Ma's syrupy red 'torture', and he warned us: "It'll sure take your hide, even after you've done a heap o'rinsin'."

Later when we moved next door to Granny, I became intrigued by the little wooden box in her backyard: "My ash hopper," she called it, "for making lye soap." It looked something like the V-shaped hay rack out in the barn, except it stood up on legs and had a little trough, or drain, coming from one end of it. Early in the fall I saw Granny lining it carefully with shucks and straw, "T' keep the ashes from sifting through," she explained, putting the tin top carefully in its place.

All during the cold weather Granny insisted on burning only hickory wood in her fireplace, saying, " 'Twill make better lye soap, y'know."

When the ashes got heaped under the firedogs near bedtimes, she'd take her little shovel and dip out some of the grayed ones and put them in a leaky water bucket on the hearth. Come morning she'd pour the cold ashes into the top of the hopper and make sure the covering was secured "to keep out th' rain water," Granny advised, adding, "ye gotta keep them ashes dry 'till yer ready to drip 'em."

And all that long winter when they'd bring a side of bacon from the smokehouse that'd smoked too dark on the ends, Granny'd save the trimmings. And when they had a ham that'd become old, she'd save the "yellered fat." And everytime they thought of throwing some old beef "taller" or rib bones to the dogs, Granny'd say, "That'll shore come in handy making the soap" — and she'd save it back.

Granny and I had just finished gathering the eggs one cold afternoon when she drew two buckets of water from the well and poured them carefully over the hopper's ashes. Then she placed a huge old churn underneath the little downspout, announcing, "Drippin' 'er off tonight, chil'. It's th' new moon; gonna be a purty day for making the soap tomor'er."

I flew home like the wind, determined to see my Granny make her infamous lye soap. My "belly-ache" went away with the school bus the following morning. Soon Mama agreed to my suggestion of helping with the soap making.

Granny's lye drippings were poured into the black washpot with great respect. A big fire was soon roaring, bringing the reddish - brown water to a rolling boil. I watched from afar as Granny lifted a rooster's bushy tail feather from the ground and dipped it swiftly in, then out of the steaming liquid. Holding the bare quill aloft, Granny announced to my Mama and the world in general: "Like I figured from the color, Pearlie—the lye's strong a'plenty to commence adding the grease."

"Stand back a'ways and don't splash it on ye," Granny warned my Mama as they readied to drop the mixture into the dangerous lye. Before Mama could question it, Granny put the fatty pork chop remains from breakfast, bones and all, into the boiling caldron.

"WHY—I NEVER!" Mama exclaimed as the lye quickly consumed everything, like a giant taking one huge bite.

After they'd thrown in all the fats they stood there an hour or more, stirring continuously with the wooden clothes paddle. And while they watched the lye eat the grease and the grease kill the lye, they kept their eyes on me like anxious hens protecting chicks from a hungry hawk.

"'Bout as thick as she's gonna git," Granny said, as the tested mixture crawled off the paddle's side like Mama's hot jelly from her spoon in summer.

The fire died down and the pot of soap cooled. Late that day two large churns were filled and taken to the smokehouse. Granny said she'd cover one with melted paraffin; the other she'd use from immediately. She began by giving Mama a generous portion to carry home.

Since Mama'd been confined to bed and Aunt Zula'd taken the brunt of the soap sent after Trillie's birth, Mama rushed unsuspectingly into using some of Granny's thin soap. First she scrubbed the kitchen floor. The rough planks sparkled white and Mama knew only excitement (since she'd used a shuck mop, not her hands for the chore).

Next day Mama headed to the wash place.

Curious about the new cleaning agent, I offered to help. I dipped my hand into the soupy soap and let it flow through my fingers and onto the heavily soiled overalls. I decided to rub them between the knuckles of my hands as I'd seen Mama sometimes do. My hands began to sting and burn; I looked to see red spots peeping through places on my fingers where skin had previously grown—I then believed all the stories about Granny's soap.

When Mama's wash flopped from the fence she walked past, inspecting it: "Was Granny's soap really the best—like she'd claimed?" Not only were the drying garments cleaner than ever before—they had also turned into sieves, with hundreds of tiny, freshly eaten holes in them. Mama drew a quick but lasting conclusion: "One'd be laying his life on the line to wager that anything was "As strong as Granny's lye soap!"

No Swimmin' in Birthday Suits 'Fore the Whippoorwills Call

I suppose that since God spoke the world into being springtime has been the season most welcomed by man. In fact most folks are so anxious for spring they start jumping the gun on the rituals every time nature tricks us with a slightly bright day after the turn of the year.

Today's false starts on spring find kids prematurely digging for shorts, buying suntan lotion, and looking at maps to the beach. When I was young they found us shedding long johns and outing petticoats, digging in the garden, and walking miles to sell five-cent packs of *Burpee Seeds* (Mama always bought all the *Marglobe* tomatoes, all the *Kentucky Wonder Beans,* and at least one pack of the giant zinnias, but she couldn't afford the seven dollars for the entire seven boxes of seeds we kids lugged home from school).

Seeing Daddy overly anxious in February to unload the seed potatoes was a mixed bag for me. The dread of the planting was lessened by the anticipation of mashed potatoes that very night. Only Mama was trusted with dissecting the precious red tubers. I always sat entranced watching her weave the sharp blade cautiously among the life-filled buds like a skilled surgeon at his awesome task. She knew how to leave the perfect number of 'eyes' on each planting piece and still save a small chunk from each potato. the remains were then used to prepare the delicious dish which we hadn't enjoyed since the Irish potatoes rotted in early fall.

In Mama's yearly rush to have "potatoes to gravel and beans to snap" for The Decorating (the all-day singing and dinner-on-the-ground at our church come the second Sunday in May) in her determination for these she sometimes got fooled by spring's spurts and reverses. A freezing night now and then wouldn't hurt the Irish 'taters, the English peas, or the onions. But let anything other than that be facing a big frost and we'd work 'til pitch dark erecting a private *Mason* jar camper over the head of every single hill—and we'd be out taking them down before the sun got head high the next morning.

My folks had their hands full on warm sunny days just keeping an eye out for younguns slipping to go barefoot. First thing you know, Daddy'd be out breaking up the garden and glance around. There behind him in the soft, cold earth would be his shadow, four-year-old Donald, trying to fit little bare feet into big brogan tracks. Driving the break plow deep into the sod, Daddy'd call, "Whoa, Maude! Whoa, Girl!" Then he'd pick up the child and say, "Come on, Squire Skimp, you're going inside to your Mama and get those shoes back on 'til the whippoorwills call."

Scientists have recently explained that it's spring's longer periods of light that do things to man's usual good sense, causing them to rush the season. I know of a group of foolhardy young boys (my brother-in-law, Lloyd, included) who, years ago got their minds befuddled one bright February day. The sight of an empty boat cascading down a rain-swollen river incited their imaginations. Quickly stripping to their birthday suits, they plunged into the icy waters and retrieved the treasure. After covering their goose pimples with their garments, they steered the craft further downstream with a piece of rotten wood and thereby established their new ownership. (But they failed to disclose their new property *or* their adventures to their elders for quite a spell).

Since over the winters we had always eaten most of our roosters, and the foxes and hawks had eaten practically all our prospective setting hens, Mama couldn't wait each spring to send off for a hundred broiler cockerels for only $4.95. When the postman brought the baby chickens from the hatchery in a pasteboard box they were in great condition. It was when the weather turned cold again that they started looking puny. It required putting the coal oil lantern in their box at night and religiously mixing two tablespoons of *Watkins* liniment in each quart of their water—all that *plus* the true arrival of spring—to get the little doodies on the mend.

Time goes by but young and old continue to do dumb things, trying every year to get the jump on spring. It just can't be done. So next February when you drive into town don't get carried away by all those bedding plants, seed packs, and skimpy clothes. Otherwise you'll be like a bunch of people I know whose new spring wardrobes always shrink after eating soup and crackers five additional weeks. Or those who pop a lot of money into the ground and are then frantic to locate 500 plastic milk jug tents.

"Lordee, Lordee, Lightnin's Hit The Barn!"

I'm convinced that Daddy inspired the National Weather Preparedness Week's first rule, TAKE COVER. At least that was the philosophy by which he lived and ruled his household. When deciding where to make the next year's crop, Daddy didn't look at the prospective house, he just made sure they had a storm pit.

If there was ever a man who kept his eye on the weather it was my Dad. Early of a morning he'd return from feeding the stock to say, "Gonna be a blustery day, might oughta keep the kids home and go to the cellar." As much as my brother Bill cheered the suggestion of missing classes, I was glad Mama'd keep right on wrapping lunches and shoo us off to catch the bus.

I minded the trips into the earth's deeps least of all when they interfered with field work. Coming in from school on a March afternoon I was glad to see Daddy walking nervously at the yard's edge, peering at the darkening sky. With luck, in fifteen minutes I'd be reading the unveiled catalog by lantern light instead of toting scrubs from the new ground.

If darkness found Daddy outside peeling his ears for a faint rumble in the West, I knew it'd be a long night. Pretty soon he'd come in and say to Mama, "It's a-making up over yonder." And she'd try to relieve his anxiety by walking to the back porch's edge and predicting, "It looks like it's scattering, Ira. Why don't you just come on to bed?".

It seemed that my Mama had shaken her fear of tornadoes somewhat. But not my Dad. Not only had he been with Mama when the storm scattered their new house into the tree tops (as they escaped with barely their three babes and their underwear)—he had brushed death another time, as a bachelor, living in Miami during the '26 killer hurricane.

So as the night sky grew more ominous he'd

eventually holler, "Get the kids, Pearlie, we can't wait any longer. It's almost here!"

And so we'd head out to the storm pit down by the barbed wire pasture fence. Daddy'd lead the way in the rain's downpour with the baby smothering under a big coat in one arm and the coal oil lantern on the other. Next we kids'd stumble along like drunken squaws with our quilt-shawls dragging the muddy ground. Last of all Mama'd pick her way by the lightning's flashes, remembering the terrible foot cuts she'd received in "the other storm". (She'd always hang behind to ensure that none of us, sulking, refused to budge from our good, dry bed).

Upon arriving at the clammy vault, Daddy'd quickly deposit the baby and resurface to stand near the doorway. There he'd coax, even beg, with love and fear in his voice, "Hurry Nonie Faye, it's a-coming. Run, son, it's a bad 'un," until the last one of us had descended the wobbly steps. Only after pulling the heavy wooden door over his head and hanging the lantern on a rafter did Daddy breath one decent breath.

As we younguns sat, groaning and complaining about the chill and dampness of the dirt cave with its frogs and well crickets, Daddy kept reminding us to, "Listen, listen—the roaring is getting closer. LORDEE! LORDEE! That lightnin' musta hit the barn!" Mama'd always encourage his faint heart, "Ira, I believe it sounded a little further off than that."

And we kids, half asleep in the middle of the night would keep saying we thought the worst had passed over and couldn't we go back to our beds. Even Daddy decided he'd miscalculated on the storm's severity the time a trapped chicken snake slithered from under the little bench to greet our arrival. (Having lived years among rattlers had taught my Daddy to fear snakes almost as much as twisters.)

A mischievous friend of mine tells of agitating his father's fear of storms as a teenager. Arriving home during a 'cloud' to find the family sequestered below the ground, Raymond decided to play a little trick. He drove his old Ford car over the top of the storm pit and sat there for a long time "revving 'er up." His father, Mr. Ed, refused to even look out for an hour or so, fearing from the 'noise of the storm' that "the whole world had been blown completely away."

Thirty-five years after the event I can now chuckle about the time my family (after I'd left home) was unable to 'come forth' from their 'earthen grave.' (The ladder had completely collapsed as they entered). The team searching for bodies among the debris of their destroyed eight-room-house found them safely in the hole and hastily improvised an escape route. That third scrape with death reaffirmed my Daddy's life-long belief in storm pits and possibly inspired the weatherman's first rule of thumb: "ALWAYS TAKE COVER."

Match-Makers: Pulley Bones and Rabbit Blades

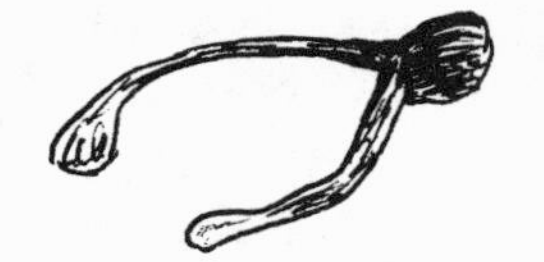

Someone has left us pondering the immortal fact, "In the spring a young man's fancy lightly turns to thoughts of love." Today's experts say this correlation in the 'rising of the sap' and 'love thoughts'—which is also true for young girls—is traceable to biological changes due to increased sunlight on the earth. I've wondered if it isn't just the realization of God's plan for relieving boredom after the winter hunting seasons have expired.

But whatever the reasons for it aside, this story explores the change in the spring-wooing rituals over the past hundred years.

On the day that the temperature rises above the seventy mark in today's world, teenage boys—and girls—push the sun roofs back on their fancy cars, turn their stereos to a deafening level, and cruise the streets and campuses, looking for the chick or hunk of their dreams. Or they walk the malls at night and flirt with a likely choice, or spend hours on the phone, or fortunes on candy and flowers.

Not meaning any reflection on the man I married, but kids of my day didn't have as wide a choice. When the March equinox occurred you did see more young people getting religious and attending church; they would then dally around afterwards 'til they found a partner with whom to walk the two, three miles home. It was unavoidable the night my first pair of high heels sank quickly into the soft gravel and I fell into the arms of John, and then expressed my gratitude for his salvation with a lengthy kiss. (It was also a month-long negotiation and bribery case of the highest sort to keep my younger sisters, Betty and Trillie, from revealing the daring rescue to my parents.)

My oldest sister, Frances, was usually restricted to courting Edward in the little side-room, called a parlor. But this became off-limits after I secretly restrained a sick kitten there overnight (planning to take it to school the next day as part of my FHA initiation). The following Sunday afternoon my sister and her beau were allowed to, recklessly, stroll alone in the meadow and carve their initials on a tree.

One sunshiny spring, when the sap was really boiling, I even connived an all-day trip with my young flame. We rode on the back of a neighbor's log truck to a "Fa-So-La Singing and Dinner-on-the-Ground." That was the most privacy we ever had, except at a community party where, during games of "Spin-the-Bottle" and "Post Office", we got to walk to the mailbox alone. (But I knew Daddy was watching the door and clocking the time so we stepped right quickly).

But as discreet as courtin' couples were back then, once in a blue moon you'd still hear of someone meeting their mate in a dark rendezvous. Why, just recently a lady revealed she'd met her hubby forty years ago on a church-sponsored coon hunt.

I suppose it has long been natural for young folks to become impatient to know who is in their future. In my Granny's youth they wondered who they might get to kiss the next fall at a corn shucking. It was decreed that if a fellow, during such an occasion, came upon an ear of red corn he was granted the privilege of kissing the girl of his choice.

My Grandma Nancy was anxious to know whom she would marry. So one spring, at the age of 15, she engaged with her friend Viola in a scheme that would, reportedly, reveal the vital information. They cooked a "Dumb Supper."

Together they prepared the meal, in total silence. Every task was completed in unison, while walking and working backwards. For instance, each plate that was placed on the table had to be carried by both girls, with their hands behind them. If everything was done perfectly, they had been told, their future husbands would come and eat with them. As the meal neared completion the sky began to darken, and with it, their hopes for their 'mates' appearance. Thunder rolled, lightening flashed, their faith waned even more. But just as they sat to eat their guest arrived with great flourish . . . an old black cat, frightened by the storm, jumped, screaming, into the middle of their table!

Girls of that day had another chance to see the face of their Would-Be's. They could drape a long rope around their neck and walk at noonday to an unsheltered well of water. After removing the well's cover and throwing the rope into the depths, the man's face could be seen in the ripples below.

My mother tried neither of the above tricks but about the age of 16 she could stand it no longer, so she tried to "get a vision of her future husband" through the "Rabbit Shoulder - Blade Method." Taking the blade bone of a rabbit she stuck nine straight pins into it. She then put it underneath her pillow and waited for a dream. And, sure enough, that night she saw a "man standing on a pedestal, wearing an overcoat." It was approximately six years later when my father, wearing an overcoat and standing on large stone blocks outside the county courthouse, first asked my mother for a date.

About the only advance notice I ever received of my future wedding status, was when, as a child, we pulled the chicken's 'pulley bone' to learn who would marry first and who would have the prettiest house.

When the sap rises and the young peoples' fancies lightly turn to thoughts of love in this modern age, they do not have to depend on unscientific methods such as pulley bones and rabbit blades to reveal their future choice of life mates. They can just dictate the characteristics of their 'desired,' right down to the size of their teeth and the length of their hair, and can arrange to meet them by way of computerized matching-hearts clubs.

When Joe Cut Short The Rooster's Outhouse Reign

Spring is the time of year when every country woman worth her salt is marking fertilized eggs to put under her clucking hens. But you can just count me out—I'm too humane to try it.

Now I realize I've deprived my children. They've never thrilled over seeing newly-hatched doodies become dry and fluffy. They've missed the discipline that came into my young life while breaking a dog from sucking eggs, cleaning out a hen house to start a garden, and saving enough soft feathers to make pillows for my hope chest.

The physical growth of my offspring hasn't been what it could have been if I had taken the chance, set hens, and had chickens in the yard. They would have had more stamina from eating home-grown-brown eggs ("chicken fruit," as Daddy called it). And their legs would have been stronger, frightening chicken hawks from near the yard or tracking down foxes that stole roosters from low limbs at night.

The intellectual wisdom of my children has been thwarted. They have grown up thinking that the ultimate in a meal is a little Rock Cornish Hen with succotash stuffed in its cavity. They've never known the thrill of eating an 'old dominecker' whose neck they've rung and taken gravel from its craw.

I just pray that my kids can forgive my failure to provide these experiences by setting hens. I just never had the heart; everytime I was tempted to do it I thought again of the gruesome path that chickens have had for years on both sides of our family.

First there was the handicapped chickens, needing crutches and surgery, that Grandma Shirley had in her yard. Seems after the old hen stole her nest one early spring, a flash flood overflowed the ditch banks and swept her eggs away, topsy-turvy. My Mama and her young siblings retrieved them for the grieving, expectant hen. When the chicks pecked forth from the shells they had all sorts of physical deformities—short legs, crooked necks, and stubbed toes—with which to face the cruel chickens in the barnyard.

My children's father, Joe, came into this world with a grudge against fowls, I do believe. As his mother's prized hatching of 14 little white leghorns emerged from underneath the house one day, tragedy befell them. The 10-year-old Joe hunkered near the wall, waiting, with a heavy stick in hand. After the proud mama hen had paraded past, Joe began to—take aim, ready, strike; take aim, ready, strike; one by one the doodies fell as they marched by. When the hen sensed something wrong and turned to look, her entire brood lay dead in a pile. The vengeful boy thought it served her right—the way she ruffled her feathers, clucked in anger, and flew at him whenever he tried to play in the yard. (And when Joe's mama saw the sight, reportedly, more than chicken feathers flew).

Ole Chicken-hater Joe was hard to change, however. Another day his target was a prized rooster, the granddaddy of many a chick, the king of the barnyard—and of the outhouse, too—or so the old bird thought. But when Joe got his *Red Ryder* air rifle from Santa Claus he put a stop to him—killed the big feller right in his tracks. He'd had enough of being in a hurry to get to the toilet and finding that old rooster always in his path, ready to flog and spur him if he dared pass.

Chicken cruelty has followed my family into this decade, as well. Not many moons past, my sister Sue was the guilty party. The 'fowl play' came as she helped her daughter with a science project, "the miracle of hatching eggs in a modern incubator." Fearing for the warmth of the developing embryos during a power outage, my sister decided to put the eggs into the gas oven and turn it on "warm" for "just a second." The rest adds to our blighted history—Sue laid the murder on the distracting phone call. But that couldn't restore the chickens nor give Crystle a passing grade in Science.

My neighbor up the road just called. She's marking eggs with pencils. Soon she'll be placing them between the fluffed feathers of a clucking hen and the soft straw in a box. It's an age-old ritual of potential life and joy. I hope my children will forgive the fact that I never got the nerve to share the wonder with them. I just knew that chickens never stood a fighting chance in our family tree.

When Daddy Whistled To The Whippoorwill

Nearly a quarter of a century's passed since with earthly ears and eyes I knew my Dad. Yet in daily circumstances I see and hear him constantly. A couple of weeks ago—a friend in telling of her hard ordeal of teaching grandkids the art of 'dropping soda by young corn'—in her telling of it, I again heard Daddy's voice. And recently I faltered—having ice cream with fried fish? Why, hadn't Daddy clearly warned, "Eating fish and drinking sweet milk together will kill ye."

I watch tall dads and short sons heading out with poles. It becomes Daddy again, young son Donald in tow, bound for a fishing hole. Or I imagine that tall, lanky talker, spinning again a tale of youthful fishing adventures along the river banks.

And when comes autumn and the first days of squirrel season, the memory wounds burst open wide. The worn-thin strap on leather hunting pouch and marks upon his trusted 12-gauge-iron speak still the testimony of his passion for the sport.

The weather man gives out a warning clear: thunderstorms and possible tornadoes for the night. It is my father that I hear—hand arched above his eyes, scanning the horizon dark—"A cloud is in the making and it don't look good."

As much as these things bring Daddy to my mind, they don't hold a candle to 'the coming of the Whippoorwill'. Now I don't mark its coming by the calendar. It's always between the time when you have to go inside early to escape the night's chill, and the time when cotton needs to be chopped.

It's the first whippoorwill call of the year—coming with its mystifying sound (sometimes happy, more often like a funeral dirge)—that resurrects my Daddy once again. Every spring it comes . . . and it happened again just a few nights ago. When the call came recently in the evening's twilight, I forgot the clothes I stood taking from the line.

The clear lyrics swept away four decades. I was a child again, sitting on the stoop of a weathered farmhouse. My Daddy, tired and du from the fields, silenced us eight as he answered the fowl.

He drew forth from time-trained lips the clear voice of the bird, like a perfect echo from our porch. Back and forth they called, daddy with the bird taking turns. Nearer and louder sounded the feathered one until it flew to garden's edge. And then, upon our fragrant lilac bush, was fraud revealed and bird ties with the man released. But family ties remained, drawn closer still because we lingered there on sweltering night to hear the whistle of our Dad.

Daddy whistled not only in response to Whippoorwills. Leaving the kitchen for the long hard day ahead he'd make a song; behind the plow when sun beat hot and mule did disobey, sometimes I'd hear him at a tune, or trudging homeward in the night's first breath. And then when bedtime drew so near, he'd find the strength to trot a child upon his knee and whistle yet another merry melody.

The seasons come and the seasons go, and things continue to remind me of my Dad. But nothing can compare with turning back the clock as when in spring the Whippoorwill I hear. And now, when comes that clarion call, I pine not only for my Dad. I pine for families of this day, for dads with time to whistle to the Whippoorwills and children stilled with tilted ears to listen when they do.

(Written as a memorial tribute to mv father, Mr. Ira W. Porter, formerly of Gordo and Northport, Alabama.)

I'll Not Let 'Em Commercialize Poke Salet

It seems that nothing old and sacred is safe anymore; my heart's crushed over recent desecrations just for a quick buck. I think I can survive it, however, if they just won't go commercial with Poke Salet.

For a beginner, take the raising of catfish. Now catfish is to us oldtimers what caviar is to the rich, a delicacy to be relished only occasionally. I believe catfish was originally intended as God's reward to young boys who sat, hours on end, holding a cane pole, enduring the chiggers. Or to grown men, like my Daddy, who would yearly defy the mammoth mosquitoes of the river swamp to hook one giant blue cat for bragging a lifetime. Or to a few teenage boys reckless enough to defy the law by 'ringing up a few' with an old-timey telephone.

But just look what the money-grubbing folks have done. They've dug ponds in every corn field and stocked them with baby catfish. And they've fed 'em out of sacks 'til you couldn't get one of them to nibble a redworm if your life depended on it. These so-called farmers have let the fish get so fat and lazy, never having to swim in search of bugs, till it's necessary to pump in extra oxygen just to keep them breathing. And instead of catching the fish, like God planned, they now *harvest* them. And every time you go to the grocery, thousands of catfish are staring up at you from the meat case. The delicious summertime treat has been degraded until the familiar now breeds contempt.

Just look, if you will, at what has happened to biscuits. This is the bread that was intended to be eaten reverently, at mamas' or grandmamas' tables. A food so special that the angels would fain have dwelled among us for the chance to eat them with spic-a-bat gravy. And yet biscuits have now been reduced to a mere snack food, something to be grabbed at every deli, quick stop and hamburger joint. And all because of the power of the almighty dollar.

I read where they've analyzed the nutritional value of May Pops and are now pushing them, dried, in health food stores throughout the nation. Their hybrid plants can also be ordered from seed catalogues to be grown indiscriminately. Congress should act on this immediately and set aside huge sums of money to assure that the May Pop will continue to grow, undisturbed, in only its natural habitat. Spring just isn't spring if one can't pause along the roadside to make a little nightclub dancer from the May Pop's purplish-fringed blossoms. Or summer just isn't summer if a brother can't frighten his sister with a loud pop made by quickly stomping the firm green ball. And the insides of the ripened yellow fruit should definitely be reserved as nourishment for those harvesting crops in the fields.

Scientific improvements in fruits and the year-round marketing of them have made those 'volunteer' peach trees and wild plum bushes growing along old roads attract fewer and fewer youngsters on hot afternoons. And paper shell pecans have become so accessible that today's folks seldom bother to chase over hills for hickory nuts. Home - grown persimmons, eatable before frost, have rendered the boy no longer a contender with the 'possum for the orange fruit in the meadow.

My paper's headlines boldly proclaim, "Banker Sees $1 Billion Potential in Muscadine Market." It then proceeds to tell of the plans for taking this "gift of God to those who loiter on fall days along dirt roads and creek banks and for those who sometimes climb trees to shake the grape-like berries to the ground for eating or making jelly or even a pie"—the article tells of plans for "turning the muscadine into a giant industry" thus destroying one of the earth's last, rare simple pleasures.

Now while there might be a little to be said about all this commercialization—about it making it possible for the boys in the city to enjoy the country pleasures; I take a different view. I think it's up to those of us left in the country to guard the sacred vestiges of rural living so the city folks'll come home again. Just knowing that cocks still crow in the morning, bitter weeds still grow in the pasture, and Johnson grass in the garden—why, those alone are enough to keep man humble and make him yearn to return to his roots.

But if there is any one thing in particular that makes me want to go back to my roots at granny's table it's the sight of the Poke plant raising its tender leaves in the early spring. I then think of granny's wisdom, knowing just how far down to pinch the young green tufts in order not to get the poisonous white roots. Then, after pare boiling the plant she'd pour off the liquid and scramble the cooked Salet with eggs in a skillet for a main dish. Or else she'd mix it with turnip greens for a vegetable or season it with salt and bacon drippings to make a salad. Anyway granny fixed the Poke it was a delicacy fit for a king.

I'll have to concede that I've lost a round or two on the May Pops and the biscuits. And I've swallowed hard and tried to accept the refinement of catfish and muscadines. But if those money-hungry merchants want a fight like they've never had before, just let them start getting ideas about the commercialization of Poke Salet in these parts!

Blackberry Pickin' On Rattler Ridge: A Self Survival Test

Acclaim was falsely given to one recently for being the first woman to make it through an extreme course in self-survival. Mama made it long ago, and dragged half-a-dozen kids along to boot. The only difference as I see it, the late endurance test was referred to as a commando camp whereas Mama called her exercise "Picking Blackberries on Rattler Ridge".

One thing I gathered from the news report was that the woman had volunteered enthusiastically for her pain—even paid for it — as a means of self-realization, actualization, or some such tom-fool-rottery. There was no such freedom of choice in Mama's case: she made the annual trek to the briar patches for family food; we went because she said so. The only time anyone volunteered was the year four-year-old Betty kept following, screaming to go. Mama said she was too young, and when all pleadings failed she placed the child in the nearby smokehouse.

My oldest sister Frances, whose lot it always fell to mind the house and tend the babies, was to let the youngun' out as soon as we all disappeared around the curve. It was a bewildering sight that met Frances' eyes when she lifted the wooden latch and swung open wide the door; the frustrated kid had vented her animosity by scrambling a dozen precious hen-eggs in the cool dirt, near where Mama had them refrigerated in a little woven basket.

My daily paper quoted the *new survivalist* on the importance of proper food, clothing, and weapons of defense. Mama thought of those things too. Instead of C-rations, beef jerkies and granola bars, however, *we* made out on cold biscuits and berries, with a few bugs and spiders clinging on for protein. Our pure water supply reached 200 degrees the time I forgot and left the rag-wrapped Mason jar sitting in the boiling sun.

When it came to clothes—Mama'd squeeze into Daddy's second pair of overalls, me into Bill's patched dungarees, and the smaller kids'd put on feed-sack britches that had straps and a bib. Long sleeve shirts to make us hotter was a rule of the day. My brother Bill got the raveling straw hat while the rest of us were 'protected' with bonnets (the kind with lots of cloth down around your neck, invented by someone bent on smothering children to death at an early age and thus exterminating the human race).

I read where the modern day mercenary - in - training told of avoiding enemy detection by rubbing herself all over with dirt. Years ago I passed up the equivalent—to saturate myself with rank meat grease and sulfur, choosing instead to meet the chiggers head-on. I also had trouble identifying with today's hero when she told of how exhilarating it was, knowing the enemy was close at hand—and being able to eventually outfox them. (Of course, SHE was armed with knives, bayonets, and hand grenades.)

We knew our enemies were out there also. The rattlesnakes ALWAYS beat us to the good blackberry patches. First we'd poke around in the lush, tall bushes with a long stick. Then we'd holler "Sic 'em!" to old Drum, Daddy's redbone hound that was as good at treeing rattlesnakes as he was at squirrels. He'd plunge fearlessly into the millions of briars and begin barking. We'd stand back and pray. Pretty soon he'd come out bringing a dead rattlesnake, bigger around than a man's arm. But many-a-time, Drum'd been wounded in the battle.

When that happened, one of us'd pick our old

friend up and tote him home. We'd feed him lots of fat meat and lay him in the cool crib. He'd swell up and be real sick and we'd think for sure that time he was a goner—but he always made it. (That is, he made it through fourteen rattlesnake bites only to be killed off by the postman's car.)

But once our dog had cleared the air—and the bushes—of the snakes, we'd commence picking the berries. Now it seemed like every year Mama'd locate a patch that was as virgin and prolific as the trees in the garden of Eden must've been. The briars on the Rattler-Ridge bushes were as fearsome as I figure the flaming sword was—the one that rotated at the East Gate of the Garden. (I always did feel like those sharp needles were a sign from God, that He originally intended the blackberries for the rattlesnakes instead of us.)

Sometimes we'd pick berries the entire blessed day. We'd pick into the little blue boilers, the medium lard buckets, and the large syrup pails. Then we'd empty those into the galvanized water buckets, the enamel dish pans (with the mend-its on their bottoms), and the moss-covered wooden bucket we'd borrowed from the well. And only occasionally would Mama let us pause to eat a biscuit, drink some hot water, or wipe the sweat with our big bonnets (although we dawdled enough that she picked four times the berries we did).

The emergency shelters that were discussed in the contemporary hardship story—well, it was rare indeed when we'd be permitted to recover from our continual sun strokes under a nearby shade tree. And the "talked about important medical attention" *that* lways came later for us. It always came the next day as we kids picked briars out of each other's fingers and red bugs from our own legs, 'nabels', and other places I can't tell.

When we got home with the berries we washed them several times then cold packed them into jars. Next we put them in the washpot, insulating each jar carefully with an old discarded quilt. A fire was then built and the berries were canned into the night. Those to be made into jam were spread thinly and left outside, covered with cheese cloth until another day.

By the following noon we'd have them finished, standing proud—50-60 quarts of berries, canned for winter, not counting all the jams and jellies. And once more it seemed as if we'd made it through our self-survival course with flying colors. Well—if the fatback I was then rubbing on my chiggers and the red fingernail polish I'd stolen from my sister and secretly dabbed over each 1,324 of them worked—well, if this happened we would, indeed, have all survived another year of berry picking on Rattler Ridge.

(I Believe) Mama Could Make A Silk Purse From A Sow's Ear

(Written in honor of my Mother, Pearlie Porter, of Northport, Alabama).

I believe the only thing that Mama's never sewn is a silk purse from a sow's ear. I have no doubt that she could—and probably someday will—make that also. She was practically born with a needle in her hand, was "wasting precious WWI thread" sewing doll dresses at six, and had pieced a quilt top for her hope chest by nine.

From the age of 21 she was sewing silks and brocades for the wealthy in the city until the deepening Great Depression took her to a farm in the country. There she turned the wheels of her treadle machine many years, staving the cold and nakedness from her ever-growing family.

During the 30s she often converted men's old trousers, given by relatives or friends who didn't sew, into skirts or jackets for her brood. When she 'came by' an entire frayed man's suit she was a master at eliminating the worn seat and the holey elbows. From it she could make a nice 'coat suit' for herself, or—more likely—a stylish overcoat for one of her girls.

When Daddy got employment with the WPA Mama splurged and ordered 10-yard remnant bundles for $1.00 each. They contained, primarily, serviceable cottons but there was always some lovely piece—silk, organdy or dotted swiss. The latter she transformed by adding appliques, embroidery, or tatting into go-to-meeting frocks more beautiful than most had seen.

During the harsh winter of '39-40 Mama performed one of her outstanding "Make and Do" tricks. It was Saturday night. All the family was in bed except her. Making one last cover-check she thanked God that the three sleeping daughters had warm coats for the winter. But her only son's frayed jacket, too small and also much too thin, stabbed her conscience. Unable to get it from her mind she silently vowed, "By granny, I'll make him one right now" and immediately attacked the task.

Taking an old wool skirt which, years before,

had been her husband's pants, she ripped and turned the garment inside out. With flat irons and a dampened brown bag she pressed the pieces thoroughly. Shifting again and again the catalog-page pattern pieces she cautiously cut the coat. Pulling her machine nearer the embers and the coal oil lamp, she sewed into the night. It was almost the beginning of Sunday when she finished the fingerwork and lovingly placed it by the boy's bed. As she laid her tired body to rest she was satisfied, thinking how warm and proud Bill would be with an Eisenhower jacket like his friends.

For years the magic-maker scrounged every available guano sack and changed them into bed and bath linens and underwear. They were bleached and softened by the hot sun, the May dew, and the boiling black pot. When tie-dyed they became decorator fabrics for making curtains, bedspreads, and dressing table skirts for her teenage daughters.

The frugal lady even once used surplus burlap bags, leftovers from my Uncle Dock's logging operation, as batting inside old-clothes coverlets, quilting them hastily on her machine to warm her family of ten.

She was my guide when I won a 6th grade 4-H dress revue. The winning garment came from 25-lb. flour sacks, dyed yellow, with intricate drawn work for the yoke.

After WWII Mama's machine had a boom-time. Small printed feed sacks became little dresses and tiny shirts; large florals meant full broomstick skirts for us older girls.

After almost 25 years my mother returned again to sewing for the public in the city. Soon she rediscovered the thrill of working with expensive fabrics. She made many bridesmaid and evening dresses, and wedding gowns, adorning some with elaborate bead work. She put her scissors to altering a mink coat and sewing bicentennial flags for a town. She also customized costumes for plays, cheerleading, and dance routines.

Looking upon her sewing ability as a gift from God for serving others, she has helped women adjust to the reality of a mastectomy by fitting them patiently with prosthesis bras. She has guided the ladies of her church in making dresses for orphans and baby gowns for overseas missions. She has designed and sewn special clothing for persons dwarfed and twisted by accident and disease. She has honored friends' requests by making shrouds for their deceased. And even now she regularly supplies tiny dresses, caps and booties to the local hospital for dressing premature stillborn babies.

Through the years she's stitched her way into the hearts of children, her own and others, by making enough stuffed animals to stock a zoo. At Christmastime assembly-line gifts roll off for her 50-odd family members: BBQ aprons and mitts for men, housecoats for ladies, train conductor suits for young grandsons Christopher and Kerry, puppets, crocheted afghans and pillows . . . the list is as endless as Pearlie's sewing thread has been for most of her 80 years.

Mama has 'retired' many times—but still she sews. We keep urging her to slow down but I expect that she never will 'til God calls her home. And sometimes I wonder if even then she'll break the habit. If God calls her first, it wouldn't surprise me in the least to one day find her just inside those pearly gates, with all the angels lined up, being fitted with new spring wings. Or to find Mama busily sewing the last big challenge—making a silk purse from a sow's ear.

A Mess Of Betty's Beans'll Cost You Plenty

I'd considered myself as nostalgic and sentimental as the next one until my recent experience with my sister Betty. My younger sibling purchased a century-old house, with land and outbuildings. The only complaint she had about the whole deal was "the way the owners modernized the place down through the years."

She told me, at the time of her purchase, that the owners had already planted a garden large enough to keep a good sized county in food for the summer. So it came as no shock when she called early one morning asking, "Wanna see my new place and get yourself a mess of beans right quick?"

"You bet," I agreed. I was hungry for some fresh beans and it'd sure beat paying that high price at the grocery and wasting my day at the check-out.

As we pulled in front of the country place Betty hollered, "Before we pick the beans I want to give you just a glimpse of these beautiful hundred-year-old logs." She started directing me to a pair of coveralls to slip on, a crowbar to work with, and one end of the front porch to begin prying paneling from.

Four hours, three wasp stings, and ten blistered fingers later, anyone driving past her door was able to get not only a glimpse, but could see the entire hand-hewn exterior once again.

"Think we better get the beans and head back?" I asked faintly.

"Yeah, I reckon," she sighed, "but first just take a gander at this loaded plum tree. What jelly they would make for Ray and Diane!" After the fifth basket of plums was in her car trunk I grabbed my bean basket and made a bee-line for the garden.

Betty cut me off at the gate. She just couldn't be satisfied 'til I took a quick peek at the boards she'd spied underneath the bedroom rug. One old carpet, three linoleums and an ample padding of '49 Country Gentleman magazines later, we were able to walk barefoot on the naked wood floor of a century past. (As I pulled five splinters from my feet I began to wonder about a sister who appreciated such a floor.)

Next we resurrected an old table and long benches from the barn and scrubbed them down. We found a broken ruler and measured for an oilcloth. Betty had a fit over four odd-shaped dishes that she found in the smokehouse. "Just made to sit the legs of my pie safe in and keep out the ants!" she screamed. Then she put me to scrubbing the rust off a metal gadget. "To rake out the ashes from the woodstove," she reminded.

By the time we finally made it to the garden I was so tired and hungry that I, like the Prodigal Son, would fain have filled my belly with the husks from the bean pods—if Betty had just given me a chance. But she decided I should dig half-an-acre of potatoes with the shovel—before they rotted. And then she convinced me to strip my white petticoat into tiny strips and tie them at 12-inch intervals along the mile-long wire holding up the youngest beans. It would frighten rabbits from the patch on moonlight nights, she claimed. (At this point I'd have sacrificed most any garment I was wearing just to get my beans and head home.)

When the beans were finally picked she thought the garden should be watered and insisted, just for old-times sake, we disconnect the pump, draw the water from the well, and put it around the vegetables by dipper-fulls. We ended by sprinkling on the bean beetle dust as the night dew began to fall.

After only three days of bed rest I was able to snap and cook my beans. You'll never find better beans. And neither will you find anyone more generous than my sister Betty is. So if you're hungry, give my sis a call. I guarantee you she'll give you some fresh vegetables—and show you her country place as well. But don't say I didn't warn you—a mess of Betty's country beans'll cost you plenty!

Sisters Of The Heart

They were not blood born. They came from different parts and different ways of life to become wedded wives of brothers. Hard times drew them close physically then great sorrows came to make them sisters-of-the heart.

The Great Depression could first be credited for the bonds they formed. The early thirties found the faithful brides seeking refuge with their husbands on the family land. There they toiled beside their men, locked in a struggle fierce to keep young families afloat.

Sometimes Lula'd walk, small brood in tow and "patching" in her arm, the long downhill road to Pearlie's new frame house. And on occasions Pearlie'd make the upward climb with three small babes, to chat with Lula for a while. As children played with pots and pans and empty spools, the women worked and talked. Pearlie'd sew on buttons and make the holes in Ira's new sack shirt, and Lula'd ready up the school clothes with hot flat irons from the fire.

But often Lula and Pearlie'd not make it all the way up or down the hill. They'd stop mid-way at "Granny's" and visit there, in the old homeplace, with her and "Grandpa Bill." This was about as far as either could go during the winter of 1935-36; they were both heavy with child. And they were glad to gather there, to spend time with their ill father-in-law, the one with whom they shared a deep, understanding love.

When Pearlie's son was born, Lula was one of the first to make it down to see the child and share her sister-in-law's great joy. She also shared her friend's deep pain a few days later when the doctor said what Pearlie'd known; the child was ill. He was too starved to reclaim in those unlearned days.

The little graveyard mound was still fresh-turned when a tornado struck in the midnight hours. The morning light revealed the devastation of the house that Pearlie had called home. That day also brought more devastation to the hearts of Pearlie and of Lula. The dear father-in-law, who'd made them feel such a part of the Porter Clan, and of whom they'd often talked—that morning Bill slipped quietly from this life. The girls - grown - old - so - soon embraced and softly wept.

Before the calendar could show another month Lula knew her time had come. But her travail failed to bring the long expected joy. The child was born, so still—without a breath. Pearlie came; they hugged and quietly cried.

The friends across the hollow, Mr. Willie and Tilmon, and other neighbors, built a tiny box. They put in padding. Next they lined the pine bed with the white birdseye cloth from Sears-Roebuck that Pearlie'd planned to diaper Little Robert with. Some women friends pleated ribbon 'round the edges to give a softness to the harsh reality.

Then Pearlie and Lula had to go on with life. They were content to show the love they had for their menfolks by working by their sides, and bearing other children, and taking care of all of them. Sometimes they took a respite from the fields and gardens and they sat together, shelling peas in their aprons and talking of their living, and of their dead.

And every spring they broke the white 'cane' from the yards and put it in fruit jars with water. They then added the running roses from the fence—the pretty little pink ones with the thorns that reminded them of their lives there—lovely at times, yet with such sharp, hurting edges all among the flowers. They took the bouquets to the graves down by the church on Decoration Day; each knew the agony the other felt. Forever they were bound as blood; deep sorrows had made them sisters-of-the-heart.

When "School's Out" Meant "To The Field" Not "Beach"

Millions of kids now count the hours in May, anxious for the last school bell to ring. They have the luggage packed, the reservations in hand, and the cars idling when the clocks tick down. They can't wait to frolic at the beach. And—weeks later—if they do return home, summer for them means only freedom, phone calls, and pizza parties. They are separated from their books but not their friends nor fun.

I know it dates me, but I can remember when kids cried at the *very thought* of "school lettin' out". And back then the last day of school was nothing short of a *wake*. The young and the older were sad because they would miss their friends and their fun. The youngest girls would miss playing jacks and jump rope; the youngest boys, the swapping of knives and marbles every day.

The older set would miss meeting, between periods, in the hallways—waiting for the last teacher's exit so they could squeeze hands, or—if they dared face death—to give a quick hug. And sweethearts'd miss riding together in the back of the school bus with fifty little taunting kids staring down at them, ready to tell the whole world if they even *made eyes* at each other.

Without cars or telephones, summer in my youth definitely spelled separation. But the main reason grown girls (and sometimes, grown boys) cried on the last day of school was the certainty of the long, hot weeks in the fields.

In fact, older boys would become a scarcity around school from March onward. They often had to stay home, as did my brother Bill, to assist in breaking up the stubborn sod. Walking behind two mules, steadying a 12" steel beam plow for ten hours, especially in a new ground, would put muscles on a young man—and kill an old one. (And it'd also put about a quart of dirt in either's brogan shoes.)

If the soil was broken while wet and a rain didn't soon follow, the section harrow would be the next thing my brother'd use. With a big rock thereon (or maybe jumping on top himself), he'd spend a day just busting up clods, preparing to plant the precious seeds.

I can remember when we were considered rich folks, owning both a fertilizer distributor and a planter. The latter would automatically put down either a little constant row of cotton seeds or would periodically drop three, four grains of corn. After Daddy layed off the rows with a shovel plow it was Bill's job to come behind with the guano. And then Daddy had to double-back and plant the seeds. If these jobs took place on a spring Saturday, I had to tote buckets of 6-8-4 and seeds to keep the distributor and planter filled and humming.

It was always Daddy's objective to help us recover quickly from the depression brought on by the last day of school by having the cotton ready for chopping and the corn for thinning. He figured we wouldn't cry as long if we made the transition that very afternoon, from our new last-day-of-school dresses to our field bonnets and sharpened hoes.

The June sun always beat mercilessly on our heads as we fought to keep the morning glories and cockle burrs from choking and rooting out the little plants. It was no wonder that as we tried to thin the cotton to only three, four every hoe length we'd sometimes accidentally cut down every single stalk. And it was also no wonder that our efforts at resetting the rootless plants were discovered within the day. The wilted cotton was easily spotted as Daddy followed closely on our heels, throwing dirt around the plants with a small shovel and sweep.

I always welcomed a rainy spell in June; it meant time home from the fields. And yet it spelled misery later when the grass grew as thick as hair on a dog's back. For when that happened Daddy wouldn't be able to cover it all when he ran the top harrow on the row's high ridge near the small cotton or corn. Or, if the crop—and the grass—was a little larger even the gee whiz (a side harrow reportedly invented by our neighbor, Mr. Tommy Goodman), wouldn't get the grass. It meant that we'd, for sure, have to go back and blister our hands hoeing out the stubborn stuff.

I was happy when Bill didn't have to plow and could help with the hoeing. For one thing, he was fast. And for another, he could break up a hot day by naming all the airplanes that flew overhead. He could tell by the whirr of the engines, long before it came into sight—or at least when it was only a tiny silver glint reflected by the sun—whether it was a twin engine P-38, a P-51 Mustang, or a B-27 cargo plane. And when the giant birds *did* fly low enough to read the lettering, Bill had always called them right! (I guess I knew back then that my brother was destined to become a military man.)

When we worked the patches near the house Mama'd send the young'uns to the field a couple of times during both morning and afternoon with a jug of cold water from the well. But when we worked the back forty we would take a gallon of water with us. As soon as we arrived, we'd find a shady spot at the end of the long rows, dig a hole and bury the glass jug with its precious liquid. In the afternoons, especially when the ground was dry and dusty, the water heated quickly.

Sometimes when we complained about the warm water Daddy'd say, "Cold water's not good for you when you're hot. Drink that hot water and go on."

But I saw Daddy change his tune about swallowing hot water one day. And I also got a glimpse of what the Apostle Paul meant when he said a lukewarm church was such a distasteful thing to God that he would "spew it out" of his mouth. My revelations came the day I pretended to be sick, went out to the rows' end, drank water, and played around. I made some dolls with May Pop blooms and fanned with some large cottonwood leaves. (And started stinging all over from the furry leaves—as punishment, I supposed). Well, I forgot about burying the water and left the glass jug in the middle of the hot sunshine when I returned to hoeing. Later that afternoon Daddy sent me to bring the water. He unscrewed the lid, took a big mouthful, and immediately spewed it out. (I think we got to knock off early to get decent water and I'm not telling what else I got.)

Now July Fourth was more than a national holiday to be celebrated at our house every year. It was also the date Daddy set for having his cotton and corn "laid by". It became my dream also, for by that time of year it was so hot dropping soda around waist-high corn that it was easy to get the picture of Hell Fire that the preacher always tried to paint.

While I know I missed much as a youngster by never realizing the thrill of summertime beach trips,

I question whether today's teenagers experience anything near the excitement I knew during "laying-by-time". When I saw Daddy pass up the wooden Georgia stock and choose instead the 12" steel beam to bust out the corn middles I got on an emotional high. I knew he would throw sufficient dirt to support the roots against strong winds and bury all threatening grass as well. My time in the fields with the hoe was ending for another year!

When last May and the end of another school year was upon us, I spent some time pondering the impact that a summer in the cotton and corn fields might have on today's youths. I can not predict all the ramifications but of one thing I feel most certain. It would definitely result in an attitude adjustment toward their haste at seeing the last day of school draw near!

My Brother'd Never Vote For A Mule Day

Yanking on a stubborn roto-tiller cord these days is enough to make folks wish for the olden days when all they had to contend with in the garden was a gentle ole mule. It's also the kind of thing that makes groups get nostalgic, forget the bad times, and plan to honor the endangered species by some sort of festival called a 'Mule Day.'

My brother and I discussed this trend recently. Now we recognize that mules played an important part in the history of our nation by pulling cannons and taking men and supplies into battle (when the horses had better sense and refused to budge). And we're fully aware that our family'd have gone hungry many a day if mules hadn't pulled the plows at our place—but to accord the mules their own national holiday? Well, Bill for one feels this is taking it a mite too far.

Now I believe if Bill could've just remembered gentle Ole Pat and the way they quietly shared the cotton rows when he was 12, he'd have quickly stood with the mule lovers. But there was Pat's mate, Frank, who clouded Bill's mind against the cantankerous critters. Oh—Frank would walk the straight and narrow when Daddy held the lines. It was just the young boy that he took advantage of.

Bill was in the wagon the first time Frank showed his wild side. He and Daddy had driven over the mountain to a little mining town to sell vegetables door-to-door. Late in the afternoon they turned the empty wagon toward home. Their pockets were stuffed with I.O.U.s (from hungry people Daddy couldn't tell "no") and a little cash. Daddy went inside the Mercantile for coffee, sugar and flour while Bill sat waiting, letting the tired mules catch their breath.

A boy on a 'wheel' came whizzing past, almost brushing the sweaty harness. Scarcely had the bicycle cleared Frank's eye when he bolted headlong, taking Pat and scared - to - death Bill in one swift sweep. Remembering Dad's warning not to yank too hard on the worn - thin lines and too scared to holler "WHOA", Bill rode helplessly, full speed ahead, behind the lopping mules. A kindly gentleman stepped suddenly from an old pickup and bravely stood in the middle of the road. Frank pulled up and quickly stopped, just as abruptly as he'd started his day's big run.

The second time Frank split was when our sister Sue lost control of a car tire she was rolling for fun. The abandoned tire came bounding at top speed just as Frank rounded the wooded trail; he lit out, plow stock and all. Bill ran as fast as a barefoot boy could, fearing a wounded mule who'd have to be shot. But it was a compassionate tree this time that grabbed the sharp steel plow, settling frenzied Frank back down to earth.

Another time Frank ran with a ground slide laden with enough cabbages to make sauerkraut for a German army. Cabbages lay shredded all over the hillside and hollows. Once Frank even dumped Bill. It was a Sunday afternoon, during an off-season. Bill was riding him through the woods, dreaming about entering one of the many caves around those parts (but too fearful of rattlers and bobcats to ever really chance it). Well, Bill was riding along at a pretty fair clip just dreaming of it when — BAM!!! Frank had stopped dead in his tracks, slinging Bill headlong from his bare back, over his head, and into a brush heap. Old skittish Frank had suddenly seen a white rag dangling from a bush.

Another day Frank ran off with a harrow behind him, but Bill and I didn't blame him that time. We'd gone alone, early that morning, over to the far off field on Pea Ridge. We rode over in the heavy two-wheeled cart, just Bill and me, taking the harrow for busting up the clods and taking our lunch of corn bread and cabbage which Mama'd cooked at breakfast. And we made sure we didn't forget to take the water.

Now we didn't just *have to* take water when we worked over on Pea Ridge. The field ran alongside where the old man was always out plowing his ox. And he'd always call, gently, "Waaaaiit, Saallllly", and dig the hand-hewn wooden plow into the ground. Then he'd say to us, "Come on up and get some cold water from the well." And when Daddy was along we'd go and get a drink — the coldest I've ever had. But we weren't going that day. Bill and I didn't want to risk seeing the man's wife and having her put a spell on us. But she did it anyway, even though we rode past fast, hiding down inside the deep rumbling cart.

Bill had just finished unhooking the single tree when the old woman came toward the field. She was dressed, as always, in a long black dress. And, as always, her long stringy grey hair hung wildly down her stooped back and over her eyes. And she carried five or six cats in her arms, with 15 to 20 others milling around her feet so that she could hardly walk. As Bill hooked the last trace chain to the harrow this old witch, as we called her in secret, approached us. Frank split—we didn't blame him; it was a real good excuse for Bill and me to split, too. But God overcame the evil spirit that day, we thought. As soon as all three of us were deep within the woods Frank stopped again, once more as gentle as a breeze. And we had escaped the witch.

All the time that Frank was pulling those capers Pat was the ole faithful, dependable one—maybe not as strong as Frank, but she was always there. Well, to be perfectly honest, though, Pat did have her quirks. For one thing she was ticklish about her ears. You couldn't just ease her bridle on, pinning her ears back as you went, then reach up and pull the ears out gingerly, one at a time, like most mules and horses let you do. No Sireee, Bob! Not on Pat. You had one quick shot at it and you'd better make it good if you wanted to bridle the girl up that entire day. (Now as a boy of 12 Bill just couldn't do it. So when Daddy wasn't around Mama did the honors. Being a woman herself she learned to outfox Pat. She'd pop that birdle on and pull the ears through with the same quick jerk of the hand, all before Pat knew what was "coming on").

But Pat's main problem was she loved Frank too much. She wanted him always by her side, or at least within her sight. And as long as he WAS nearby, leading the way, she'd go most anywhere and do most anything. Why, if Frank was along carrying someone, she didn't mind Bill riding her all the way into town. Even when she came in from the field, tired, she wouldn't object to having little Doug ride her from the watering trough to the barn—not as long as Frank was there, plodding by her side. But let Frank be out of her sight—then try to ride her away from the house and you were in for a heap of trouble. She just would not go in the opposite direction of the house and barn no matter what you did; she refused to leave her beloved.

A neighbor boy, Major, boasted one day that HE could do it. He said he'd get on Pat in the front yard, without Frank anywhere in sight and ride AWAY from the house and barn, without any trouble; he'd bet on it. And he put up a quarter to prove his conviction.

Well, Major led ole Pat past the front yard where all of Mama's flowers and shrubs were in full bloom. He started leading her out the little road, away from the house. Then he leaped astride her bare back, dug his heels into her sides, and hollered, "Yiiiiiii, Pat, let's go!!!!". Pat whirled around, made one big jump over Mama's large crepe myrtle bush and took off to the barn. She left a broad path of pink crepe myrtle blossoms strewn between the house and the barn like a flower girl gone wild running down the isles.

When Pat pulled in by the barn gate, right beside the fence where Frank was eating hay, Major was a strange looking sight. He was pale as a ghost as he dismounted with both trembling hands filled with hairs he had snatched from Pat's mane. Meekly he turned to Bill and said, "Come on over in a while and I'll give ye yer quarter." At that time Major would have gladly gone on record with Bill as being highly opposed to honoring the four-legged creatures with any kind of recognition, let alone a National Mule Day!

Liniment Pie And Brunswick Stew: Celebrating The Fourth of July at Granny's

Celebrating our Nation's birthday at Granny's as a child filled my heart with love for family and love for country. It was back when sons and their wives were willing to move home, take over the family farming, and care for an aging mother like my Uncle Ferman and his loving wife, Aunt Gertrude, did for my Granny.

Granny was feeble but she was still valued highly. She was valued for her ability to shell peas, rock babies, and make the most delicious teacakes the world had ever tasted. She was also esteemed for her fierce patriotism and her great talking ability, traits which she exhibited best on the Fourth of July with all her kith and kin gathered about her.

Early on the morning of the Fourth, Granny's four adult sons started the fire under the big black washpot they had placed in the shade of the mulberry trees near Granny's front porch. Granny would voice her opinion—right and left, as the big pot started filling up for the Brunswick stew.

First she would say to my Daddy, "Ira, t'weren't no need'n killing three o' your roosters". Then to another son, "Gray, reckon you might as well throw both o' those pig shoulders in".

"Pearlie, your butterbeans're sure filled out good", and "Gertrude, you beat *all* growing giant tomatoes", she'd say as the daughters-in-law dumped heaping bowls of fresh vegetables in with the cooking meat.

The men always brought a rocker for Granny and placed it in the circle of straight chairs where they gathered to tend the fire, stir the stew, and talk. They would also sample the keg of lemonade made with the lemons their city brother, Purve, had brought and with the ice Ferman'd packed in sawdust out in the smokehouse.

"How's your corn coming in the new ground?" someone would ask another.

Then almost in unison a third would inquire, "Both your milk cows going dry at th' same time? That's too bad," they'd sympathize, shaking their head slowly.

"Planting sorgham cane again, eh? Law, 'member how that 'twas Sam's favorite crop to help Pa with—'fore he went off to th' war."

The brothers and their Ma'd talk back and forth and would, eventually, always speak—in reverent tones—of Granny's son and their brother,

Sam, whose body had been shipped home from France after after World War I. And when we gathered during the war years of the 40s, they would talk quietly of my older cousins off in Europe, of Buck and Everett, and of their prayers for peace and the safe return of their sons.

While the mamas worked in the kitchen—cooking up huge amounts of fresh vegetables, breads, and desserts—the cousins played. Many years Sara, Louise, and I found a quiet room for dressing dolls and playing house. The young boy cousins, Ted, Jim, and Roy, used ropes from the barn and ran around lassoing each other, yelling, "Hi Yo Silver, Away!"

Adolescent boys played in the gullies behind Granny's house, sometimes swinging on kudzu vines like Tarzan in the movies they saw in town on Saturdays.

The oldest boys and girls—among them William, Frances and Elizabeth—gathered in Granny's living room and took turns winding by hand the old Victrola and playing its indestructible thick records. It made them mad when we kids came in insisting they play such things as "She'll Be Coming Around the Mountain When She Comes", and—the one we liked best of all—the one called "Laugh It Off". In the latter, the singer got started laughing and laughed hysterically throughout almost the entire recording. We young ones always rolled on the floor in giggles; the teenagers became furious. Just when we were to the point of blows, Granny always came toddling down the hall and restored peace once again. It required only her gentle presence or her quiet reminder, "The Fourth is a time of peace, chillun'; peace in the land of freedom—bought at great price".

When the outside table was piled high Granny asked Uncle Purve to "turn thanks". He thanked God for the food, our health, and our great land. And then he asked God to help us keep it free.

I reckon the only thing that I can ever remember that was not perfect about the feasts at Granny's was my cousin "Duck's" vanilla custard pies. And this was just one particular year, because they were usually my favorite and the best of all the desserts.

The story goes that on the third of July Granny had been rubbing her rheumatism with the tall bottle of black *Watkin's Liniment*. She walked through the kitchen and placed it on the counter where "Duck" had assembled her pie ingredients, including a tall dark bottle of *Watkin's Vanilla Flavoring*. The rest is history, including the tales of how those who ate the pies were relieved of their rheumatism for some time after that.

After dinner at Granny's everyone gathered around the small, stooped lady, talking a little—but mostly listening. When asked, Granny would spell from memory, page after page from the *Blue Back Speller*—"b-a-c-k, back, p-a-c-k, pack, r-a-c-k, rack . . . and on and on—spelling, pronouncing, spelling, pronouncing. And she would recite old poems from her school days, some humorous like, "I Jumped Up 'Fore Jaybreak". And she would exhort us on right living, quoting from the Bible as she did. Then a strong message on the value of liberty and justice for all was sure to follow.

Eventually the wonderful Fourth of July at Granny's had to end. As each family started to leave, Granny got her little black leather purse with the golden chain-handle and she waited by the front door where we all came to hug her. She stood there passing out one-dollar-bills to each and every one, adults included, regardless of how they protested. And she said, "Bye and God bless ye Now don't rush the team on the way home, Ira And, you younguns, don't ferget to give thanks fo your freedom."

When the last person was gone Granny' purse was always empty too, which was the wa Granny wanted it. You see, Granny cared not fo material things and seldom bought anything excep candy for the kids. Her only money during thos days came in the form of a small monthly pensio from the United States Government. Grann thought the money she received should be give away, lovingly, sacrificially, without thought fo herself—just the way her son, Sam, had loving and sacrificially given himself in France in ord that we might celebrate our Nation's Freedo every Fourth of July at Granny's.

Watermelons: An Endangered Species?

Statistics may tell us that the production of watermelons is at an all-time high. But I feel it's time for real melon lovers to rally round: modernization is fast stripping this summertime treat of it's true place in our lives.

If you have doubts about its erosion, just think of the way watermelons are planted today. They are planted scientifically, on huge irrigated farms; no longer are they planted as God planned—by the full moon, Good Friday, or the Almanac. The seeds planted now are hybrids, bought from giant stores, and they are put into the soil by machines operated by impersonal folks interested only in a paycheck. We melon lovers know that the seeds should be placed in a choice plot, during a joyful ceremony, by an entire family whose father has saved the seeds from a pampered seed-melon and brooded over their drying and preservation as a mother hen broods over her chicks.

Another indication of today's rapid decay is the way melons are now pulled and culled. No longer do excited children race daily to check on the largest melon in the patch, waiting anxiously for their daddy's first thumping of the same. That, plus his notice of the dying curl, helped him, in earlier years, make the happy prediction, "Yep! She'll make it by the Fourth!". And it was the daddy, all summer long, who was able to look at a melon, thump it, and tell just how ripe and sweet it was gonna be. Or if it would have a hard, white streak in the middle from too much rain. Or if it was just a no-gooder from a volunteer plant that had mixed with the nearby gourds and should be fed to the cows. (It saddens me to read that melons are now gathered solely by the calendar and are graded by computers at the rate of 40,000 pounds per hour.)

As noted above, having a melon ripe by the Fourth of July was once every family's dream and the thoughts of it fueled hard work during hot May and June days. I feel the lethargy abounding today is traceable to the fact that melons are no longer anticipated; they are shipped into grocery stores almost every month of the year. And when fresh ones aren't available, little frozen melon balls can easily be snatched up.

The mention of the melon balls brings me to another important part of this "plea to save the endangered melon". Now time was when every part of the watermelon was valued; this is no longer the case. Today's sophisticated society is interested in only melon balls or melon squares taken from the fruit's heart and placed on crystal dishes to be eaten with tiny silver forks. And the only time you will come face-to-face with the striped rind (belonging to the delicious Dixie Queen melon that my Daddy believed in)—the only time you will see it will be at a wedding reception. And it will be hewn out to resemble a little green basket with a handle and will be filled with all kinds of foreign objects like strawberries, grapes, and kiwi fruit. There will be just a few perfectly-rounded balls of red melon therein, as if to imply that God has gone to portioning out watermelons in rounds instead of rashers.

Yes, today's modernists are just desecrating and wasting summer's main joy. The watermelon was originally intended to be eaten by the rasher (or slice), with the juice dripping off one's chin. That is, unless an entire family stood around eating out of the two halves. This latter custom left the empty 'boats' intact for scraping and squeezing the last bit of the meat into juice for drinking. Sometimes this heavenly liquid would be drunk straight from the rind; other times it was strained into a jelly glass, removing the meaty pulp. And somewhere during this happy time the family was supposed to tell jokes and ask riddles about watermelons like:

"I was down in the field and found
a little green house.
In it was a little white house;
In that, a little red house.
And in the red house were a lot of little boys.
What was it?"

Or:

"As I was going over London Bridge,
I met old Granny Gray.
I ate her meat,
I drank her blood,
And threw her skin away.
What was she?"

At our house, however, part of the last ditty didn't hold true; we didn't throw the skin away. Well, we did toss the green of the rind to the cows in the pasture. But that was all.

Sometimes the white part of the rind was cut into pieces for making watermelon rind preserves or pickles for the cold winter days. But more often we spent hours of a hot afternoon carving false teeth from the white. Occasionally we cut nicely-shaped pearly dentures but usually our imaginations ran rampant and we created the forerunners of today's Draculas. With our frightening tusks in place we chased each other 'round and 'round the yard as though we were blood-sucking vampires.

Of all the watermelon parts, none was more important in bygone days than the seeds. Now I'm not referring to those carefully saved for the next year's planting. I mean the "run of the mill" seeds that we vied for every day when we ate melons. They were the medium required for the tame "seed-spitting contests" that we sometimes had. More often they were ammunition for our "seed wars". When Daddy forbade us to spit them back and forth as we stood, eating, around the old shelf underneath the well shed, we hoarded the seeds into piles.

Then when the melon was gone we stuffed our cheeks like chipmunks with the black slippery things, and we dived behind big trees or around the corners of the house. Next we ran back and forth, quickly spitting one seed out like a shot from a cannon, then darting back, or else making a wild dash for someone's hideout and spitting a volley of seeds before they could pucker up. Unmindful of germs or such, we delighted when we landed a slick seed in the face of a sibling—of Doug or Shirley Ray—or a visiting cousin. Defeat was conceded only when one's seeds were depleted or when you got so tickled you had to spit your entire arsenal onto the ground rather than swallow them.

But the fiercest use of the watermelon came at the end of a big family reunion. My brother Bill and his cousins'd start snatching up the rinds and running, breaking them into pieces as they went. We girls took cover and screamed from inside the windows.

"SWASH!" would go a juicy piece up beside Bobby's or Troy's head. Turning quickly, their bronzed muscular arms would bring a loud "OWWWWW" as a large pieced rested on Bill's naked back. Soon it was time for the juice - soaked cousins to leave. They sat in the back of the wagon attracting all sorts of flies and bees on the homeward journey.

But times have changed—for the worse, I think. And the watermelon's caught in a downward spin. So, Old Time Melon Lovers, can I count on you? Will you help me stem this tide to take watermelons from their rightful place in summer fun?

Mama Cured Me On Canning

Everywhere I go during July I meet ladies with sagging shoulders, sunken eyes, and purple hands. "Puttin' up'll kill ye," they all begin. And while I listen guiltily, they unwind their tales of woe: "Between six and twelve last night I put up 150 ears of corn, the day before it was three bushels of pink-eyed purple hulls (the hands extend as proof), and the day before that it was homemade vegetable soup—28 quarts of it at the final count. Last week Horace took his vacation and together we stood 105 beautiful quarts of green beans, 35 jars of apple jelly and 15 of cucumber pickles on the shelf in the pantry." And on and on and on they go, while I'm slinking lower and lower in my chair.

Now I'll concede that there's lots to be said for summertime puttin' up but I'm just not the one to say it. I've always had my craw full just puttin' up with the kids out of school and Joe home for longer hours. But I think my real aversion to summer food preservation had its deep roots in my childhood.

Mama maintains our canning exceeded one thousand quarts only one year; my memory wants to disagree. Mama was a good gardener; she also believed wasting just one string bean was a mortal sin. Furthermore, she was ahead of her time on knowledge of vitamins and such—and insisted we can the entire spectrum of available nutrients for the cold months. In order to help achieve this, we'd start even before the garden came in—by picking and canning every blackberry in sight.

The thing I dreaded most about summertime canning was washing all those fruit jars and zinc lids. Having a small house and a large family, we stored our empty jars in an old shed where they became inhabited by bugs, spiders and crickets. It was my brother Bill's chore to bring the jars out, pile them into a washtub and cover them with water from the well. It fell my lot to do the actual washing of the jars. Since being blessed with the smallest bones in the family enabled me to extend my hands through the narrow jar necks, I was privileged to daily share the tub water with the floating dead bugs (that Bill deliberately left therein) 'til my hands shriveled up like so many dried apples.

Mama was particular about all her canning but she took special pride in her green beans. First, she'd insist on removing the strings herself and then we kids'd chop them on a cutting board or the metal counter of the kitchen cabinet, always squabbling over one particular knife which cut better than the others. Seems we'd wash the beans forever before Mama'd heat them in a dishpan and then scoop them, steaming, into the scalded jars. Sometimes she'd trust us with the adding of one teaspoon of salt—which we had to level with a knife for accuracy—in the top of each quart jar. After closing with Ball dome lids and rings (the zinc ones with the rubber bands were reserved for the tomatoes), Mama'd put the beans into the pressure cooker.

Kids were allowed in the hot kitchen during the pressuring process only for emergencies like rushing in with a fresh load of stove wood. (The pressure cooker was regarded in those days with about the same respect that the atom bomb is today.)

When the cooked beans were taken from the canner they were put on a clean folded guano sack. It was a sad sight come morning if there was a jar on which the little dome on the lid had failed to indent. This meant they hadn't sealed, had spoiled overnight, and others must be canned to take their place.

Space fails me to tell of all my childhood canning memories. Of the days of piling wood around Mama's washpot and the old cut-off steel drum for outside coldpack canning of kraut, tomatoes or peaches (trying to keep the house cooler for sleeping at night). And it was outside that we scalded tomatoes and beets for what to me was the most fun of all canning tasks—the zipping off of the beet skins. I remember the condiments we helped in making: the beet, Indian peach, and cucumber pickles. The gallons of tomato catsup and many jars of chow-chow we loved on peas. Just recalling now the giant bowls of minced onions required for the former two activates anew my overworked tear ducts.

There was the shredding of cabbages for churns and barrels of fermenting sauerkraut. Of the years when excess kraut and canned tomatoes were sold to the school lunchroom or exchanged for lunches for us children. Of the huge peach tree which provided us with bushels of delicious Elberta peaches every summer. And of the apple trees which provided me with the impetus needed to stay slim as a rail (Mama ran me to death puttin' out and takin' in the sliced apples as we tried to dry them every summer in spite of daily July showers).

My sister Trillie reported last July that her summer had just 'peaked.' Just when she thought for sure she'd run out of Mason Jars she made another wonderful discovery. Not so with me. All those childhood years of wondering what other kids meant when they referred to time away from school as 'summer vacation' made deep inroads into my thinking. The damage was deepened when Mama's old washpot broke in half, thereby sealing the fate of the outside coldpack. The knell sounded for pressuring when my presto cooker blew all over the kitchen, in a split second painting my walls the color of the sweet potatoes I was cooking inside.

I am now in total agreement with the Wise Man in the Bible who said there is a time for all things. Notwithstanding the delicious naturalness of home-canned and frozen foods, for me the time of the necessary "home puttin'-up evil" has passed. I early on taught my kids to cry for corn and beans with a picture on the can. Their first little ditty was "Campbell's soup is good food."

A few years back I thought I might have somewhat of a problem, though: Joe presented me with a 20-foot Coldspot. I soon found a solution. At the earliest mention of food from the garden I rush out, eager to fill my freezer. I've discovered that for the paltry sum of $15.75 I can fill the entire thing to overflowing with day-old bread. It frees me up all summer and the birds sure have a heyday come fall.

Needed: Government Help On Making Brushbrooms

Every now and then I run across a listing of the many free pamphlets and brochures available from the U. S. Government. Just for the cost of a postage stamp you can receive detailed instructions on how to build everything from a beehive to an outdoor toilet. There's just one glaring gap I've discovered in the help that's needed: *The Making and Use of a Brushbroom.*

Now I'm not a graduate of an agricultural college but I've got sense enough to see that summertime rain often creates a nationwide grass problem. It results in an alarming increase in stress on American citizens as a whole: kids have trouble locating their baseballs, dads have trouble positioning their hammocks, and moms have trouble keeping the stuff cut.

Of course I'm aware some folks, whom I refer to as Lawn Freaks, gloat over the entire bad situation. They're the people who, since Day 1, have dedicated their whole lives to the growth and care of their lawns. They've brought in topsoil by the truckloads, spread on a type of guano referred to by city folks as plant food, and hauled in ready-made grass. It's high-priced grass, I'm told, cut up in squares like abody'd cut up a big pone of cornbread before putting it in front of a bunch of kinfolks. Well, they've laid these little grass squares side by side, all over the front and back yard. They have grass as thick as hair on a dog's back all in one day. It's the likes of which if Mama'd woke up one morning and seen in her yard—well, she would have had us out there day and night with a dozen hoes till the last blade of it was gone and the yard was barren, fit once more for decent folks.

But not these Lawn Freaks. When they get this instant grass to going, they don't let up. They just keep pouring the plant food and the water to it. And they go around poking in the lush stuff, trying to find one little bug. Then they rush him off to have him studied and analyzed and have some poison mixed up to fit his own particular diet plan. They put out good money for mowers, and trimmers, and spreaders, and sprayers and, next thing you know, it's pills to ease their own tension.

Now I'll admit that every once in a while I get to thinking it'd be nice having a lovely green carpet outside my window. then Joe quickly reminds me that I married him for better or for worse, not for constant lawn mowing. But whenever I'm so relaxed in the summertime I feel guilty about my neighbors, the Lawn Freaks, having to use amphibious mowers with headlights just to keep open a path to the door. I get to wishing they had all of Mama's invaluable expertise on keeping her yard grass-free and clean to boot. I reckon it's high time I did a good deed for them and my country by offering to write a free government pamphlet on "*Making Brushbrooms*".

Now this leaflet I've got in mind could be real simple; it's production needn't run nearly as expensive as all those federal investigations into politicians' secretaries. I could tell how you first of all rid your yard of all grass and weeds, leaving only nice smooth dirt or sand. This can be done, I'd say, by letting adolescents take hoes to it, kids play ball on it, or leaving an influx of army worms completely to themselves. And then I could explain the brushbroom's construction process. And add a few words about it's historical importance both for cleaning the yard and for children's discipline. It could read something like this:

"A brushbroom is the part of small saplings that remain in the edge of the woods after mamas jerk off all the little switches for practicing child psychology. First, you break or cut these young trees, then tie or wire them together to form a broom similar to the ones witches ride.

"A brushbroom should be allowed to dry a few days and the leaves thrashed from them before using. Otherwise the leafy limbs will collect too much sand, making the yard trash impossible to sweep. Or else the leaves will begin to fall off as you sweep, leaving more trash behind than you collect.

One important rule to remember when

sweeping your yard with a brushbroom is: strokes must always follow the same direction." (It is poor taste, or poor something 'er other, to have marks in your yard at more than one angle, according to my Mama's rule.)

And, lastly, I'd add this note:

"NOTE: The brushbroom has proven through the years to be a very effective weapon for mamas to use when threatening rowdy, bored teenage sons who are pestering their younger siblings to death. It is believed to be much more persuasive than present day tactics such as withholding the use of the car or the allowance." (For instance, my Mama'd say: "Bill, if you don't leave your sister Nona Faye alone I declare I'm gonna take a brushbroom to you!" Just the thought itself was always sufficient in Bill's case. Of course, the threat, like all modern-day ones, was never carried to fulfillment.)

I personally think this idea has limitless potential. I figure when this pamphlet catches on it'll save the average Lawn Freak hundreds of dollars, mend countless marriages, and prevent the construction of juvenile detention centers. If the instructions should prove to be somewhat obscure, folks are more than welcome to visit my place for a free demonstration. After last summer's rains and the subsequent heavy grass growth, I took a sharp hoe to my Bermuda and made me a nice new brushbroom!

My Daddy's Pocketknife

When Daddy died he left few worldly goods behind. But Mama gave to each of us some little remnant of his life. I got his pocketknife, then placed it near my mantel's end, the way that Dad would always do at night.

That knife had been my Dad's most useful tool. He used it as he readied for the field; with it he'd scrape the hardened dirt away and loose the screws to change the plow; he'd get the pebble that was lodged between the mule's foot and the old iron shoe. And if one of us got a thorn or splinter while we worked with Dad, his knife became the gentle scalpel that was used; a quick swipe upon a frayed pants' leg was all the sterilizing that it got.

As Daddy used his gun and old cane pole for getting family food, so he used his trusty knife to skin the creatures and to scale the fish.

My Dad was never pushed enough to make him till his crops upon the Sabbath day, but often he and a neighbor'd walk the fields together on a Sunday afternoon. During a dry springtime, they'd pause often; and with his knife Daddy'd dig from the dusty soil some grains of cotton or some corn. Next he'd use his blade to cut the seeds and check the chances of the germination. And when the plants were small and the friends came upon a wilted one, my father'd dig down by its roots and find the culprit grubs. Then often as the fall came on, I'd see him splitting cotton bolls and Dad and Mr. Homer sadly shaking their heads over weevils that they'd found.

It seemed Dad talked his best with pocketknife in hand. So when a relative dropped by, and they sat in straight chairs underneath shade trees, or they just propped on the chopblock and talked around the woodpile—Dad would always, automatically, pick up a stick of stovewood or some other thing and he'd begin to smooth the splinters down. Or, if they were walking side by side, I'd see my Daddy quickly snip a weed or twig, then move along, making sideways slices from the plant.

It was this quick response with pocketknife that helped him save his firstborn son. The barking dogs alerted him to danger and he quickly drove his plow into the sod. With flying feet he ran and cut a large limb as he sped. The giant rattler, coiled, was ready for his strike at Dad's own child's bare feet. The first sure blow was all that saved the youth the deadly bite. (My Dad was no longer thirsty for the water that the son had fetched.)

At Christmas Daddy'd wash his blade and peel the apples that we got from Santa Claus. I marveled how his knife went 'round and 'round until the peel hung long, all curled, without a single break.

Although my Dad could never be called a master carver, I remember his knife most for the things he made with it for others. Before he walked the miles to visit with his "Maw" and sister Essie (who would today be termed a 'special person'), he'd take his knife and cut some tender blackgum limbs and make many 'toothbrushes' for the two. He'd make them uniform in size and length, and remove the bark a certain distance from one end of each. It was his gift of love for them; they used them when they dipped their snuff.

Sometimes Daddy'd get a limb from a squash vine in the garden and use his knife to make a whistle for one child; or he'd bring a reed from **the bottom** and make a more permanent version of the same.

On winter nights as we sat by the fire Daddy'd use his knife. "Let me sharpen your pencil," he coaxed "so you can do your figures better." Sometimes he'd help Bill and Doug whittle slingshot stocks from hickory chunks. Then they'd finish up the weapons using an inner tube (cut into rubber strips), old shoe tongues, and twine string unraveled from a sack of 6-8-4.

After Daddy'd poked up the dying fire a bit, he'd take the spool that Mama'd just emptied of it's darning thread and he'd make a little toy. After he'd notched the spool's ends with his knife, he'd thread a hoarded rubber band through the hole, attaching a match stick to one end and a small piece of crayon to the other. Then for a long time he'd amuse the smallest of our brood; over and over he'd tighten the rubber band by twisting the match stick 'round and 'round, and then he'd put it down and let them watch the little tractor crawl along the floor.

But after awhile we'd see Daddy fold his knife and lay it near the mantel's edge; we knew the happy evening had to end. And, a few years back, when my Daddy's last long night came on, I laid his wondrous pocketknife right near my mantel's edge; it reminds me of it's magic in Dad's hands.

Bills Truck Wagon:
Go Cart's Forerunner

The paper's headlines said a go-cart reached 160 miles per hour: my brother's truck wagon beat that four decades ago. To give Bill his delayed fame, youngsters need to know that the truck wagon's speed of yesteryear was achieved with no engine. Like the unique design of today's Talladega 500, however, I believe Bill's course had as much to do with his speed as his artful buggy did. It was shrewdly engineered on a cliff side, with a 90-degree turn beside a giant oak. Nonetheless, machinists through the decades have been hard pressed to improve on the wagon's basic "I" frame. It could wrap around the oak with the loss of only one wheel and five pounds of human flesh. This agility came from a time-tested piece of discarded bridge timber plus the small hickory tree axles.

As winter's firewood was readied keen eyes kept a look-out for a smoothly rounded black gum tree. Once the right one was discovered plans for heated hearths were put aside. Dad and son rolled tires and rims, all-in-one, off the assembly with our wobbly cross-cut saw. Many more than the required four were dissected: they would sure be needed for 'blow-outs' on winning downhill drives. But sure drying and cracking of the rounds, like today's dry-rot, prevented huge stockpiling of the important racing treads. Having no awl with which to bore the holes, Bill and his friend used red-hot pokers to complete the tires from hardwood slices.

Rough lumber for the steering wheel and column was hard to come by in those post-Depression days. Often it, along with the needed nails, had to be 'borrowed' by use of a claw hammer from the backside of the barn. Once these were in place the only thing lacking on the Rolls Royce was a discarded washpan to fit one's bottom firmly into on the death-defying rendezvous. It was an extra benefit if, before adding the pan, someone removed all the little 'screws' therein. Those little "Mend-Its" attached periodically to the leaky enamel pan had prolonged its life; they did just the opposite for the life of a rider on a bumpy terrifying track.

I am living proof that a begging sister who continually hounded her brother and his best friend, Tim, was eventually given her turn. I am also testimony to the fact that such a sibling needed only one such hair-raising cruise before gladly settling into the overstuffed pine needle chair in her pasture playhouse. From the safety of the high straw walls she was then content to sit, watch, and chew a little 'pine rawsun' from a nearby tree.

It was hard to tell which echoed more through the hills—the men-childs' excited yells as they careened wildly down the dangerous slopes or the crashing of the wagon when it hit the oak. On a routine trip, nearing 200 MPH, Tim once lost control; he also lost his shirt, his stomach skin, and the truck wagon as well. I thought Sunday afternoon excitement was blown to bits.

The resourceful boys were not to be outdone. They turned to swinging out of tree tops and building a Flying Jenny. They began the latter by secretly borrowing a 20-penny bridge nail and another barn plank. After attaching them to a 4-foot stump, they again had the means for flying through space like today's astronauts.

I reckon Bill and Tim got their craw full of fast traveling and truck wagons as kids. They're now content driving sensible cars with tops over their heads. It isn't that way with many of today's men, however. I see them out testing the truck wagon's descendants—their sons' go-carts and dune buggies. I have a hunch it's like the old saying about building a better mousetrap. There's seemingly a great hunger for a better go-cart;

practically the whole world's searching for a path to Bill's back door. For the sake of old-time neighborliness I'll be glad to point the way, but when they start asking for a demonstration that's the place where my accommodating ends.

Our Gnat Smoke: The First Great American Smokeout

A nationwide event took place recently which was erroneously referred to as 'The Great American Smokeout.' The first such happenings actually took place at our house when I was but a child. They were started by my Dad and were called gnat smokes.

Of course those outside events happened in simpler times when all kinds of bug sprays, repellants and smoke screens didn't come in cans. Neither did little trucks putt-putt around the neighborhood about dusty dark sending out a poisonous fog. Not that it wasn't needed, mind you.

I have a hunch that just after Eve ate the forbidden fruit and tossed the core aside, the need for the first insect repellent arose. Probably by the time the Lord came to call her from the fig trees a swarm of gnats had already been drawn to the apple's juice.

I make these statements because one of my first observations in life was the fact that a few gnats and mosquitoes "just had to be tolerated." But the summer I was designated by Mama as the official "peeling taker-off-er" was the year my eyes were really opened to the reproductive capabilities of the worrisome insects.

That year we peeled tomatoes to make tomato gravy, tomato sandwiches (in huge, flat biscuits), and tomato soup. We canned large whole tomatoes, tomato juice, tomato catsup, and tomatoes in vegetable soup. We had buckets upon buckets of tomato peelings and pieces of decaying tomatoes. Mama gave me a choice: either clean up the kitchen or take the peelings about a quarter of a mile from the house, beyond the garden. I took the 'toting job' and made out; I sneaked the peelings into the tall grass just behind the smoke house.

Next we canned peaches, made peach cobblers, and peach preserves. I hid the remains nearby. Then we canned apples, made apple butter, apple turnovers, and apple jelly. I again chose the 'toting job' and got off easy; I put the peelings in the bushes at the edge of the yard. I piled them near, and in, the chipped fruit jars that Mama'd told me to take to the far-off gulley.

And then came the July rains. And the 100 degree weather. And then the Lord sent the 'Great Gnat Plague' and the 'Mosquito Menace' upon us to torment us and to reveal my sins to my mama and my daddy.

After supper on steaming nights we tried to rest and cool off by sitting, in the dark, on the front porch or nearby yard. That year it was impossible; the insects chewed us almost to death (and I felt that, deep down, the family blamed it all on me).

But Daddy remedied the situation. He set

some discarded rags afire and poked them down into an old leaky chamber pot. Everytime enough air got to the rags to cause them to flame, Daddy'd run quickly and rearrange the rags. This would snuff out the blaze and leave only a big, billowing smoke. Occasionally Daddy'd pick up the chamber by its bail and move it to take advantage of the shifting smoke. I think the objective was "to waft the smoke directly into your face." That way, if it didn't chase the insects away, you'd come so near smothering you wouldn't mind their bites.

A piece of wool cloth was Daddy's number one choice for a gnat smoke, but before the Great Gnat Plague summer had ended, he was settling for any kind of rag he could get his hands on. And that year we also discovered that if someone happened to be getting their head shaved you could throw a handful of human hair into the smoldering fire and, well, suffice it to say that any metropolitan exterminating contractor'd pay a fortune for the formula these days.

Taking a close second behind Daddy's gnat smokes as the 'Greatest American Smokeout' would have to be the time Bill and I smoked rabbit tobacco behind the barn. And coming in for a tight third would be the entire day Frances and I spent down at the spring—choking, coughing, drinking gallons of water to quench the fire in our throats. The two *Lucky Strike* ready-rolls we stole from Daddy's rare pack and smoked below the hill forever cured us of our smoking urge.

So the next time you hear they're gonna have The First or The Second or The Third Great American Smokeout don't you believe it. We qualified for those distinctions years ago.

Needed: A Water Witches Corp

Great national leaders have historically organized mankind into corps to relieve human suffering. Following the example of Roosevelt's CC Corps during the Great Depression and Kennedy's Peace Corps during the turbulent 60s, the President should act immediately to establish a Water Witches Corps to end the current devastation from the drought of the century.

The Great Communicator could begin with a TV appearance to re-acquaint the nation with "water witching" and tell how this age-old ability to locate moving water played a vital part in the settlement of our country. (And, if he wanted me to, I'd be glad to give a testimonial about the time we moved to a log cabin on a high ridge and—after a well-digger dug four deep, dry holes—Daddy consulted a water witcher. The man's green stick started jerking, going crazy, and twisting in his hand within a few feet of the four empty holes. Being a skeptic I hollered, "Mister, hold that stick tight and it won't turn downward." Well, he held it tight all right, tight as his strength would allow. First, the bark started to peel as the stick struggled to move. And then the triangle broke, right down the middle. It also made a believer out of me. The 'dowser' explained it as a baffling force that had pulled the instrument downward, indicating water. And, sure enough, upon digging, the pinpointed area produced an endless water supply. It was located at exactly the 30-foot level the 'witch' had predicted by computing three feet deep per pace between the stick's initial twitching and the time it pointed directly downward.

After I'd told my personal story, the President could continue talking to the nation about the need for a Water Witches Corps. He could declare how it's now up to us to forge ahead—to rise above our present stop-gap tactics of overcoming water shortages by means of national hay-lifts, adopt-a-cow programs, and human consumption of *Gatorade*. (I REALLY BELIEVE a speech like this would rally Americans behind such a corps. It would eventually restore to our endangered land a plentious supply of pure water, even during a dry summer, although it might not initially be as exciting as paying $140.00 to name a beautiful, brown-eyed animal and then calling, toll-free, to hear your own adopted cow "talk").

In concluding his national appeal, our great leader could announce that Congress had appropriated huge sums of money to undergird the training of thousands of volunteers in this recovery program designed to put "water in every pot—and plastic milk jug—around the country." He could then introduce my good friend, Mr. Victor, whom he had chosen to head up the demonstrations. Mr. President would explain that the good ole fellow is one of only a handful nationally who still makes it a practice of locating spots for good wells of water by means of a "divining rod." (He probably wouldn't mention that a prime factor in the man's selection was any would-be critics' frustration—with Mr. Victor having a Ph. D. and being a professor in a great university where he is respected).

After being appointed head of the Water Witches Corps I suspect Mr. Victor'd immediately call for all volunteers to gather in a giant peach orchard in Alabama. There he'd begin to demonstrate the cutting of forked peach limbs to be used in the great National Water Search. While cutting the 12 to 15-inch prongs he'd give out the following information: "Some claim the ability of water witching, also known as 'dowsing,' comes only through inheritance from a relative who previously had the ability. But I believe that ANYONE who will approach the task with an open mind and who will patiently crisscross the land can perform this great humanitarian act of locating vital underground water," Mr. Victor will continue. I can imagine him as he then firmly grasps two of the three prongs of the "Y" he's cut, and allows the third prong to point upward, free. He will then further explain, "Some folks disagree on using my favorite, the peach tree limb, and they choose a willow or a hickory for their tool. Either will work but the most important thing, I think, is that it be green and flexible."

If I know Mr. Victor, he will soon hasten to add: "However, some water diviners use metal rods. Why, I've even heard of modernists taking coat hangers and twisting them into ninety degree angles. By holding two of these L's pointing north, in front of him, the witcher walks across the land, watching for the metal forks to turn in opposite directions (one to the East, the other to the West). When this happens it's an indication of either the possibility of a future water well or the presence of already existing underground water pipes."

I feel sure that my friend will at some point advise the weaklings to return to their homes, citing the heavy drain of physical energy that the locating of water, oddly enough, takes from a 'witcher.' He'll also give some warnings about the difficulty of correctly interpreting a divining rod's message when the water is exceptionally deep or when standing over an area where two underground streams crisscross.

Mr. Victor will probably then announce two associates who will help advise the volunteers learning to witch in the peach orchard. The first associate will be my young niece, Angela, who watched her paternal grandfather practice the helpful craft and proved her proficiency with it at the tender age of three. She is well qualified to travel throughout this land adding a "women's lib" angle to the previously predominantly male trade. She will, undoubtedly, lead women from coast to coast to witch for their own water wells, ensuring that never again will they run short on water to do the dishes.

My brother, Bill, who as a young lad had training in water witchery from our neighbor, Mr. Tommy, will become the second associate. Having already served his nation in four foreign countries he is well qualified to become an international demonstrator in order to extend this wonderful Water Witches Corps to the entire thirsty world.

The thousands of water witching volunteers initially trained in a peach orchard in Alabama will eventually fan out across this great nation to witch for water and locate sufficient reserve wells and springs to ensure a bountiful supply of water for all purposes, including a year-round irrigation of crops even in the midst of a record drought. And then my dream will have become a reality. For just as the CC Corps eventually employed two million who built the bridges, the roads, and worked on the national forests that we are now, fifty years later, still enjoying—just so I envision that history will record, and the American people will one day observe as a national holiday, the day that the President nullified the great drought's effects by his wise establishment of a national Water Witches Corps.

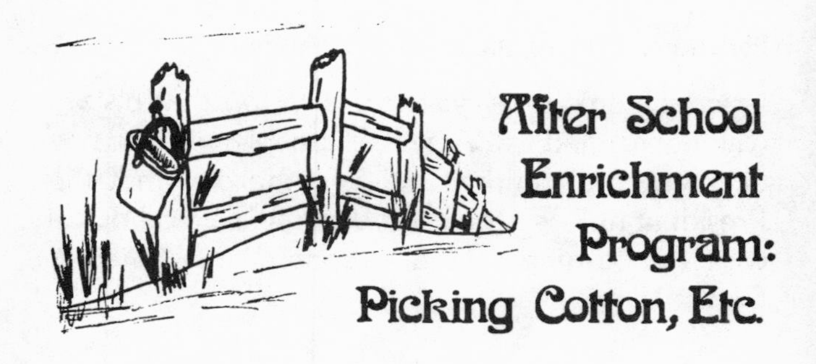

After School Enrichment Program: Picking Cotton, Etc.

Local Ys, PARAs, and church schools are offering youngsters After School Enrichment Programs; some call them Playnastics. Mama and Daddy offered us one also; they called it Picking Cotton, Etc. I can see several parallels between today's setup and the one in which I participated for many years.

Contemporary enrichment plans promise parents a lot for their money. They provide the kids with adult supervision, a variety of activities, and opportunities for growth in interpersonal relationships. They also furnish fast-food snacks and all necessary activity equipment. Their outline differs from my elders' agenda on only one point: they have added a pick-up service directly from the school door to the activity site. A convenience like that would've chopped four miles off my September walk from the bus stop to the far side of the back forty.

I am inclined to believe that the afterschool fast-food snack might have originated at our place. My folks early implanted in us the incentive to eat our sweet potato and cold biscuit as fast as humanly possible while we lit-a-shuck to join them in snatching fibers from the stalks. We felt confident also that when we arrived at the field our adult supervisors would have our activity equipment all laid out, waiting. There'd be varying sizes of cotton sacks—ranging from the long, snaky giant for my strong, teenage brother down to the little flour sack for my first grade sister.

Our growth in interpersonal relations occurred as we learned not to quibble over who got the row with the fewest saw briars and cockle burrs or who picked the row next to Daddy (since he'd always assist you by yanking the hard-to-reach bolls on his side, and even occasionally by stuffing a handful of the fluffy down into your sack, making you look better at the scales come sundown). (Permit me to mention here that we'd never have gotton up nerve to reach our 100-lb. quota as my husband, Joe, did as a youth. He added a field melon to his cotton sack for the extra weight and consequently shut down an entire county's gin for several hours).

Our after school activities took on variety as we left the field and scrambled to complete home chores before pitch dark. There were animals to feed: mules, pigs, chickens. Cows had to be milked (the number which had gone dry was directly related to how many toads we'd killed that year, some claimed. I had my doubts). Wood had to be piled behind the kitchen stove where by then Mama, who'd left the field a little early, had cornbread baking to supplement the heated leftovers and the cold, sweet milk. Our grown-up direction carried over to mealtime when we knew better than to begin eating before all were seated and Daddy had blessed the bounty from God's hands.

Our parents, like all alert planners who keep participants on their toes, provided for frequent changes of pace. As soon as the cotton was picked, the corn had to be pulled by Daddy and my brother, Bill. Sweet potatoes had to be harvested and stored, regardless of how the oozing syrup discolored and rendered Sue's adolescent hands unfit for 'holding'. There was always the gathering of late peas and okra, and on the eve of the first real frost the bringing of the last green tomatoes to ripen inside.

As though fearful we'd run out of something to do and become restless, Mama'd plant giant patches of fall turnip greens and winter collards. In the cool afternoons as we'd pick up a flat board and begin an impromptu game of string ball, our Matron'd spy us. She'd have us gather a mess of greens for ourselves and one for the "old neighbor down the way. And," she'd add, "go scratch through the dirt and straw in the 'tater hill' and throw in a few nice red ones, baking size." It wasn't that she didn't believe in fun; we just had to learn to whistle while we worked.

Our leaders, like their modern counterparts, left nothing to guesswork; they thought ahead for inside activities on rainy days. We could always change clothes quickly and scurry to the crib to shuck and shell corn, either for grinding at the gristmill or popcorn for cold nights and parties. The alternatives of threshing out dried peas and butterbeans or picking peanuts off the vines were always present.

When dire cold kept us inside, younger siblings needed tending while Mama instructed one at sewing on the Singer. Then while she called directions, we had the enforced opportunity of trying our hands at baking cornbread, cookies or one-egg cakes. And every night after supper, regardless the season or weather, there was always the one-way choice of happy banter while softening hands in dishwater. Supervised tutoring, better known as *hard hitting of the books*, then followed close to end the day.

I heard recently of a problem at one of the local After School Enrichment Centers: the director resigned after the kids grew bored with the proffered activities. The board was searching for a qualified replacement with lots of action in mind. I thought of my folks. Daddy's gone now, but I had them ink Mama's name at the top of the list.

Swap My Sears 'n Roebuck Catalog For A Video? NEVER!

There's a movement afoot to put most of the world's great volumes on videocassettes: novels, cookbooks, and catalogs. I hear tell that people are paying up to twenty-five dollars just to pop a videologue into their players, lay back in their recliners, and watch things to order. But I can tell you quick, it's gonna take more than a little cassette to take the place of my catalog.

When I was a kid the Sears and Roebuck 'cattylog' was an important thing. The book was put to uses by rural people that Sears, the merchant, and Roebuck, the watchmaker, never dreamed of when they teamed in 1887. In fact, its myriad uses by the country folk has been a symbol of their neighborliness, their family closeness, and their way of making-do.

For a long time the printed word was skimpy in sparsely settled places. The Bible wasn't scarce but it was kept up high, on mantel scarfs, away from careless hands. During school months there were the tattered 'rithmetics and readers, and sometimes— here and there—you'd find a family getting *Country Gentleman* or *Progressive Farmer* magazines. But almost without fail, you'd find the *Sears, Roebuck and Company Catalog* in every humble home.

Around the year it served as their *Dick and Jane* for reading practice, as their Webster's for learning new words and as their Brittanica for checking out the facts. Even the United States Post Office recognized the book's importance and classified it "educational matter, second class mail".

It was their *Wall Street Journal*, their index for the value and the cost of things; ordering stovepipes and singletrees from within its pages gave the older a chance to practice frugality and show their children how to do the same. Its pictures told their hopes and, its leaves, when old, became a hundred things which symbolized their resourcefulness, their love.

At our house the catalog had no special place to lay; it seldom rested from its rounds. As it passed back and forth, tattlin' might be heard, "Mama, make Sue gimme th' cattylog. She had it last and now it's my time." But more often we kids lolled under the oak in the noonday heat, laughing, sharing the big book's dreams.

"Woooo - Weeeeeeee, look'it this wheel (bicycle)!"

"Yeah, if the crops bring enough, Daddy's gonna get us one, said he would." The thoughts of it sent us again and again, vigor renewed, to fight the Johnson grass on the back forty.

Late on a freezing night our family drew more warmth from each other, and the catalog, than we did from the dying fire as we huddled, choosing the new pair of brogans that Daddy could no longer do without.

"Betty, tear me a sheet uf ya tablet paper", Daddy'd say, taking off the shoes held together with baling wire. With a pencil he then made four short lines, marking the boundaries of his heel, his big toe, and either side of his right foot as it rested on the paper. Mama figured it: the Wearmasters with "added resistance to barnyard acids for longer wear" ran $2.55, plus twenty cents for the parcel post, and eleven more for the money order the letter carrier would attend to next day. Then she put it, with the tracing and the three coppers for a stamp, into an envelope and laid it carefully on the mantelshelf.

At school they told us to read everything we could get our hands on. That often boiled down to just the catalog. When Bill was writing a report for Agriculture and needed to know the spelling of "hames", Daddy said, "Check the cattylog, son, way over in the back". And in the fifth grade the teacher was flabbergasted over my new reading vocabulary, I didn't tell her I'd spent the entire summer studying—memorizing the description of every ready-made dress in that big book.

The catalog was a priceless reference for Daddy and other country folk when it came to trading in town. Once when Daddy's crosscut bucked and broke in half (while sawing a huge pine, trying to pick up a few dollars cutting timber after the crops were laid by), he walked the ten miles to the mercantile for a new one. The owner asked him eight dollars, two weeks' work.

"Awwwwwwww, feller—I know I'm in a tight—but Roebuck's got a better saw 'n that, a Fulton Lance Tooth, six-foot-long, with their best wood handles for only three ninety-eight, plus four bits for shipping it. Can't you come off a little for a pore man?" And, sure enough, the owner obliged him and settled up for six bucks, on the penny.

Big boys, as well, soaked up the information in the book. They hid in backrooms and gasped at its pages of panties, girdles and brassieres. And they took their sharpened pocketknives and cut out entire sections of the fancy underthings and the pretty girls, and hid them between their feather beds. They came to take them out, again and again, studying, learning about life.

Nearly grown girls invited friends over. Late at night they pulled heavy quilts up under their chins and turned, with chilled fingers, the catalog's pages, seeking inspiration. The Helena Rubenstein cake rouge and the silk stockings fueled their plans for high school graduation and glamorous jobs in the city.

On the very day when one came racing from the mailbox with a brand new catalog, the creative rural souls began to do all sorts of things with the old, outdated book. It came in handy for wrapping a sheet around a cold sugar biscuit and taking to the field. There the snack was placed in the "Y" of a sapling, hopeful that mid-morning'd come before the ants crawled beneath the little dinette table for $15.99. The hot jars of muscadine jelly were turned upside down on the hardware pages near the cookstove, for cooling.

When country folk killed hogs and the neighbor who came to help forgot to bring a bucket, they wrapped him up a mess of liver and lights, and a little tenderloin, in parts torn from the old Sears 'n Roebuck book. Or they wadded the paper and poked it into broken window panes, choking out winter's killing breath. Or made fans from it, trying to cool hell's steam during a hot, dry summer. When their little books of tissues ran out, these rugged men shook tobacco from cloth sacks into jagged papers that said, "Our best Overalls". Or they sat in their toilets on the hillsides and read, "Blue chambray work shirts—good quality, 3 for $2.97."

Often several catalog leaves, glued together with flour paste, became a dress pattern, or shelf paper to be put into the apple crate nailed to the kitchen wall. Or parents helped the children transform them into kites.

Daddies showed the little boys how to make boats or airplanes with long johns on their wings. The mamas let the girls pass Sunday afternoons cutting catalog paper dolls, pretending they were the ones dressing in the finery and laying on the studio davenport (the couch their mamas had wanted for their own front rooms). Grannies taught the youngsters to cut lacy doilies from the big book's printed leaves.

Maybe you've seen the miracle of a seemingly dead fire on a chilly morning suddenly exploding with bright new flames. All it took was a few crumpled catalog sheets near the gray embers and a little fanning with some others. When crops failed, or cotton prices hit rock bottom, our year-long dreams turned dead-gray with the collards in the garden. But the arrival, in the spring, of the new catalog sparked again our flames, our indomitable spirits. And again we asked the banker to "advance us" another year, and we planted our crops, and dreamed our new dreams.

And now do you think I'd exchange a 'cattylog' that is all these things, and more—for just one measley video cassette? NOT IN A MILLION YEARS!!!

"Thankee For Some Cracklin' Bread And 'Taters"

She was just simply "Granny." Not just to us of blood but to all folks for miles around. She came to be a legend in her day. Though sun and rain has changed the shade her tomb rock bears, it has not worn her memory thin.

I knew her when her mate was gone, and years were hastening on. When toil of field and cooking for the hands had left her stooped and frail. When son and wife had come to share her load, and home, and care of Special Child called "Essie." I'd walk the lane late in the afternoon to spend the night with her and find her shoring up the outside chores. She'd shoo the hens away to let the doodies peck the corn grains she had shelled. She'd call her grown-old-child from the pastime of picking peanuts from the vines. We three would greet the warmth of kitchen's door with loaded arms of stovewood from the stack, or splinters for the hearth, or eggs caught up in Granny's apron-basket.

She'd wash up at the shelf and help Aunt Gertrude with the supper for the crowd. There were, always, the extended family of nine, an extra grandchild or two like me, and other boys who'd found the home a place for work and warmth and love. She'd fry huge platters of the ham they'd smoked, then mix the corn bread with her hands, and make the biscuits in the old bread tray. She'd open wide the oven on the hot woodstove and check the baking sweet potatoes with a little squeeze. She'd bring the butter she had churned that day and place the 'pats' upon the great long table with its benches on the sides. And last of all, she'd pour tall glasses of sweet milk and buttermilk. After her son, Ferman, said the Grace, I'd wait my turn and ask for food, "Granny, thankee for some ham, some cracklin' bread and taters."

And for dessert I'd say, "Thankee for one of yer little fried pies, Granny." The butter-fried half-moons were her gift of love to us; from peaches that she'd dried in summer. After she had sliced the fresh peaches thin and spread them out on sheets of tin to catch the boiling sun, she patched the overalls outside underneath the old mulberry tree and scanned the sky for chance of rain. She sat and watched as faithfully as 'possums watched the 'simmon tree for ripening fruit in fall. She knew we ranked her pies up near the top—right beside the teacakes that she made with ginger.

Reading her Bible and dwelling on God's long eternity had molded Granny into patience-in-the-flesh, a lot like God-come-down. After supper we'd sit by the fireplace and chat and Granny'd take the two combs and four hairpins carved from bone out of her hair and let it all come falling down. When she slowly combed the long thin silver tresses that then rested in her lap, she'd give way to wishing and recite from *The Blue Back Speller* of her day, "C-A-T, cat, R-A-T, rat, M-A-T, mat, F-A-T, fat", or tell about my Daddy and his schooling, how he'd always loved writin' and figurin' more than plowin', or she'd talk to me about The Good Lord and His Word.

Even after Essie had turned in and called, "Ma, make 'aist (haste) and come t'bed", Granny didn't rush. She'd poke the fire and place the glass eye (that she'd had since youth) upon the mantelshelf and stand there in her flannel gown. As she slowly rubbed the empty socket in her pleasant smiling face she'd say to me, "Child, don't let me forget when you go home t'morrow. I aim to send your Mama a bucket o'that good lye soap I made a while back." When she sat down again to rub her rheumatism with some liniment, I dawdled, hoping the wondrous time would never come to an end. She didn't fuss when I spilled her Navy as I sneaked a peek in her little snuff box while she went to kitchen door to "ranch my dip out and get a sip of water from the dipper." From the cozy bed I'd later watch her, like an angel in the firelight's glow, wind the ageless mantel clock so it would never miss its striking.

First thing in the morning she would comb and put her hair up in its ball again. And shortly after breakfast she would come and make her bed. While she flopped the mattress first from head, then foot, and beat and beat with hands and little fists, I'd go from one corner post to another and turn 'round and 'round the big brass knobs that stood all day and night like polished soldiers watching over Granny's feather bed. I never heard her snap a word nor even say she wished I'd stop.

She would readjust the band of rubber on the old sage broom and say she needed to "bresh up the hearth a little." And then sometimes she'd cut and cook the squirrels that were killed at woods' edge in early dawn, and make a dumplin' stew to feed the bunch at dinner. Or she would wash and 'pick' the collards and the turnip greens out at the well.

Her hands were never idle. She would pass a rainy day, as she'd say, "just piddlin'", picking hickory nuts from their hulls or pulling cotton seeds from the bolls she'd picked in tucked-up-apron at the field's near edge the day before. When the fluffy locks were clean she would card them into bats and give them to my Mom for quilting into cover for us kids.

My little Granny loved to talk and never knew a stranger. When a traveling man—an insurance collector or the Watkin's dealer—passed through, she'd say to them, "Come up and sit a spell and pass the time o' day." And she would talk, and talk, and hear the news they had, and then on them she would prevail, "We got plenty. You're sure obliged to stay and eat," or "It's gittin' s'late, why don't 'cha stay over til th' mornin'?" And when she made her rare trips into town, she'd stand around in the Yellow Front buying patching thread and the City Drug buying Black Draught and she'd talk and talk and talk. And even those who'd never met the little lady knew of her through others and they would gather round to talk with her. Everyone just called her simply, "Granny," not just those of us by blood, but all the folks for miles and miles. She had come to be a legend in her day.

Shooting Marbles and Jumping "Hot Peas"

When the old schoolhouse fills again soon it won't be a response to the principal's ringing of the little bell in the schoolyard. It'll be a direct result of my Grandpa Bill and Granny Mell taking seriously God's admonition to "multiply and replenish the earth." If there's a nip in the air Uncle Ferman'll drive over early on the day of the reunion to start a fire in the pot-bellied stove. Still sitting where I, as an eager first-grader, backed up to it four decades ago, the heater's soft warmth will once again put me to remembering. I'll think of Mrs. Plowman, the Angel with chalk on her hands who introduced me to the magic of *Dick and Jane*, and presented me with heaven's jewels (a set of water colors) for perfect attendance that year.

Maintaining the family tradition we'll do our part of the talking when we gather at the former home of the 3-Rs. My dear Aunt Essie'll ask for pictures of all the babies. Cousin Jewel will point out the hard-earth court where she and Ruth played basketball against county schools in years past. Rowena and Virginia will speak of the hop-scotch area and how we girls used our rope for skipping "Hot Peas." Jim and Roy'll remember how the boys used their new plow lines for tough tug-of-war games.

Bill and Gene will again try to set the record straight concerning their involvement (?) in the spitball fight which reportedly transpired on the spot where we now spread the fried chicken and candied yams. And for which alleged fight the substitute teacher, Miss Suzie, introduced my brother and his cousin to one of the primary purposes cloakrooms served in the educational process of that day. Those closet-like partitions were also used for impressing adolescent boys with the futility of expressing puppy love by putting green snakes on girls or throwing acorns on their tin-roofed privy during recess. Or of falsely taking another's prized 'toy' marble.

Although it was rendered unnecessary five years ago when the cloakrooms were converted to 'indoor facilities,' some of us will still brave the weeds and briars to the old outdoor toilets. We'll go after the moth-eaten textbooks, printed before Pearl Harbor but lately hauled off to share life with the frogs, snakes, and spiders down at the old john. We'll bring back and cherish the copies of the

Champion Arithmetics with their antique black-and-white illustrations. We'll laugh over the story in the Winston reader where John's deepest Christmas desire was realized: Santa brought him the hatchet he wanted to use to cut wood for Grandmother. We'll mull over the fading penciled names of classmates, friends and sweethearts written therein. (And we'll pore over those names left more permanently, with pocketknives, on the desktops from which we'll eat our family feast).

My oldest sister remembers many historically significant events which happened at the old school. She'll tell again how her teacher combatted proration back then. The delicious pies the schoolmarm baked that went, piece by piece, by selling penny guesses on mystery articles placed underneath the pie slices. My sibling's hunch one day, a fruit jar rubber, won for her a cut of the smooth chocolate with meringue.

Frances will also review for us how the term 'Field Trip' originated from that very school. It was the year the entire student body went on a 'field trip,' taking sacks, lunches, and all on schoolbuses to a sick neighbor's field to pick his cotton.

Next, pointing to the small stage, Frances'll remind how this was the exact spot where, in third grade, she made her acting debut. If coaxed she'll again recite the poem and demonstrate the horrible facial contortions she was required to make because, "Jimmy Jones He Teases Me".

We'll miss my Uncle Perve and my Daddy,

Ira, being there to bless the bounty. We'll miss Aunt Lula's smiling face reminding us struggling Supermoms of how she, with 13 kids, sold Blair products nearly five decades ago. We'll give thanks that Uncle Gray, although in his 80s, is here, again outdoing all the fancy city foods with his hot corn bread, fresh turnip greens and good pot likker. Folks will scramble for Aunt Gertrude's caramel cake, Aunt Vennie's good ham, Aunt Dess's fried peach pies and my Mama's chicken 'n dressing. The food and fellowship will remind us of days, and nights, when the entire community gathered with a bond of love in this schoolhouse for Box Suppers, Egg Hunts, and Halloween Carnivals.

After our family lunch, friends will drop by. Then we will gather around the old piano. We'll think of the friends we went to school with here, who are no more, and of the relatives here last year but not this. And we'll sing "*Will the Circle Be Unbroken?*" and "*I'll Meet You in the Morning.*" Then we'll sing some of the oldies from school: "*John Brown's Body,*" "*Home on the Range,*" and "*Down By The Old Mill Stream.*" After we've cleaned up the tables, laughingly designated the 'No. 1 Talker of the Day', and hugged and kissed around several times, we'll take our leave once again of the old country schoolhouse. And as we go we'll remember how we left years ago—running, pigtails flying in the wind—to return, carefree, the following morning.

When Hound Dogs Chased The Hens In Peace

I like the lazy days between the heat of summer and the cold of winter. When all I must now do to make the seasonal change is twist my thermostat from "Cool" to "Heat," I think of other hectic years. I see the endless chores of childhood's 'bringing-in' and 'shoring-up' that got us ready for the season dire.

Of course the cotton, corn and other crops were brought in early from the fields. But smaller, more subtle things were destined for a change as well. The least of these was not the bringing of the bucket and the washpan from the shelf. The time for this was told by Dad; when morning's early splashing at the back porch's edge brought briskness too intense.

Daddy never cared for timid rinsing of just hands. On summer days he'd roll his sleeves and lather past the elbows and cover all his face with frosting white. Then, dipping deep for several times, with large cupped hands he'd carry half the contents of the pan to splash again upon his hair. And taking the comb from off the warped board fastened onto the porch's rail, he'd stand before the broken piece of 'looking glass' nailed to the wall and sleek his handsome black hair back before he entered for a single meal. (It was as much a part as the Grace he always prayed before we ate).

But winter's coming changed the way in which my Dad washed up; he'd do it gently then, standing inside the warmth of kitchen for a spell. And so at last the hound dogs chased the hens around the corners of the house without fear of having Daddy always sling out his water from the pan just as they drew near.

When signs of frost first hit the air we lined the long enclosed hallway with Mama's flowers from the front porch shelf. They were an odd lot there: those which survived the year before and clippings from the neighbors near and far and all in syrup buckets, chamber pots, and chipped earthen pitchers that had at one time sprung a leak. When the flowers' leaves were falling on the floor we picked them up and carried them once more. On their last move we took them down to share the darkness of the cellar with the spiders and the toads.

The late onions and the red peppers were gathered in and tied about with colored strings. These brightened Mama's kitchen from nails high upon the smoke-stained walls.

The sweet potatoes were snuggled down more carefully than a baby for his daily nap. First there was the heaping of the soil into a mound. Soft hay or grasses formed the bed and coverlet where the red 'rooters' took the rest they had to have to sweeten up their juices for our supper meals. Next, corn stalks covered over with more dirt formed a tepee with a tiny hole to let in air but ward off rain and any snow that fell. It was my daily task to take some 'taters from the side, then close with great precision and much care the hole I'd made within the "hill."

The wild sage brush from the one field that had 'laid-out' that year was cut and bundled for storing in the loft. This must for sure be done before the winter rains and winds had time to rot and spoil the grasses we used for making brooms to sweep up all our floors. Mama let us gather with her butcher knife instead of twisting down the straw like most folks did; the twisting left our hands with cuts and gashes from the sharp edge of the outside leaves. The butcher knife in winter months was also used to 'preen' a bundle for a broom, to get the extra husks and fuzzy foliage from the broom sage stems.

The missing window panes that in summer only let in welcomed air and caused no stir when a playful youth with a slingshot knocked another out . . . now were holes that against the north wind's breath must in some manner be closed. In some sparse years no glass ones could be bought to fill the gaps; we borrowed from the windows on the back to make the eyes that greeted visitors all clear. The ones in the rear were then cut out of wood or pasteboard from a box and fitted tight to hedge against the freezing blasts. Or old pillows were stuffed into them like big fat ladies into small society chairs.

When the last of the windows had been closed in and the quilts piled up six to every bed, we knew that we were almost braced for winter's blow. When wood was stacked behind the kitchen stove and near the fireplace, and on the porches both—when splinters of heart pine lay within the kindlin' box, and the washpan had been brought in from the shelf—when all these things were finalized we feared not if the shucks upon the corn were thick and doomed us to a winter bad and long.

Turkey Talk Hotline: A Shift from Olden Holidays

My body and will power just weren't coordinated to accommodate all the extra cooking and eating that goes on from mid-November 'til mid-January. If it were something one could get accustomed to gradually, such as learning to talk, then I'd have had the chance in childhood. Mama'd get the feasting off to a bang by cooking her fattest rooster, with all the trimmings, for Thanksgiving dinner. The results for me became obvious right after the desserts; I could hardly squeeze into my brother's extra pair of overalls for our family trip to gather wild nuts.

Youth and the regimen of the day were on my side back then, however; by night the patched britches hung loosely on my frame. Taking Bill's dare and crossing the creek on the slick footlog scared part of the extra fat off me. Running up the hill to the treasure trees (discovered by Daddy while hunting) burned away a little more. The warm fall afternoon of play-work finished off the rest.

The wild chestnut tree had opened her prickly burrs and dropped two nuts from each into the thick carpet of brown leaves before we arrived. Her nearby relative, the chinquapin (chinky pin) tree, had done the same with her clusters of tiny nuts. It was as if the beeches had entered into a conspiracy with the deer, squirrels and wild turkeys to hide their delicious meats from our eager grasp.

Using quickly devised rakes of fallen limbs we tossed the leaves to-and-fro, revealing the secret caches. As the mahogany - colored jewels came into view happy squeals echoed off the deep woods' trees to be heard only by our troop of ten. Then cautious hands filled mouths, pockets and pails while avoiding the fruits' spiny envelopes. We older girls had to harvest with one eye on the ground and one on our mischievous brother. He was sure to catch Mom and Dad watching the young ones, then toss (by way of an attached stem) an especially sharp burr toward us. Making contact was like my imagined petting of a porcupine.

Satisfied that we'd hardly left one chestnut there for seed, we kids ran ahead of our elders to the hickory that bore the largest nuts of its kind in those parts. The last gold leaves tucked their chins in a sort of mockery. It was as if they laughed over the effort we'd spend on wintry days, pausing inside a shed to crush the hulls with rocks and tediously pick the tasty morsels with a hairpin or a nail. But they didn't know that Granny waited then—for many to be cracked and placed nearby her fireside warm. They didn't know the patience that she'd have in picking meat from stubborn shells for days on end. Nor could they know the joy of grandchild stopping in, near Christmastime, to share a slice of memory cake, stacked between with hickory nuts by Granny Mell.

The abandoned house place up the road with it's huge old walnut tree, became the last stop on our long ago Thanksgiving jaunt. With black-walnut filled tow-sack on Bill's strong back, and youngest son dozing piggy-back on Dad's, we rushed in home just as dark closed down the day. Hot tomato soup and fresh cornbread where whipped up in a flash; there had been no leftover rooster to warm again.

The birds we bake for feasting now have multiplied in size while families have shrunk. Youth and the regimen of the day no longer side with me; I'm middle aged and TV is the after dinner thing instead of running through the woods to gather nuts. And when night now closes in on holidays, I'm stuck, with skin-tight overalls and turkey piled up high, to last a month. But help is finally on the way!

It seems that for every crisis in life there's now a toll-free hotline where one can call and talk. When we're in the middle of the holidays it is sure a relief to know one such line has been established to help folks deal with eating leftover turkey. (After the per capita consumption of the big fowls doubled in the last ten years it was deemed an absolute necessity. Computer printouts tell us, however, there's still only an eleven pound per capita consumption in a given year; right here and now, I'm going public with my apologies to all those folks whose portions I've been eating.)

There is one problem; I know that when I call that turkey hot line I'm bound to start an uproar with them over today's caloric content of poultry. They're gonna tell me it's about as low in calories as poke salet and I'm gonna tell them how I ate left-over turkey from mid-November 'til mid-January one year with a net gain of 20 pounds. But, regardless of the certain squabble, I've posted that Turkey Talk number right by my phone. If that turkey carcass stares out of that refrigerator at me as long this year as the one did last, then some crisis volunteer is for sure gonna go sleepless. (Oh—by the way—the number is 1-800-323-4848 just in case you need to make a call yourself.)

Corn Tops, Fodder, and Pea Vine Hay

I had a feeling it was an omen of hard times for the farmers: last spring my neighbor paid good money for Johnson grass seed and sowed it in his field. I also had a feeling my Daddy was turning over in his grave, remembering his life—and mine—devoted to killing the pesty stuff. I figured Daddy was pretty upset, also, over seeing so much fodder, corn tops, and pea vine hay going to waste in recent years. "Waste not, want not," he always said, making sure we brought ours in.

Now for you young modern farmers whose notion of foliage for your animals is giant hay rolls clad in plastic ponchos, the following is a primer on fodder, corn tops and pea vine hay, or, "how to feed your stock during hard times."

Fodder is the dried blades of corn that farmers of my youth fed their mules and cows during the cold winter months. It came not on trains nor planes during hay-lifts, but it came from corn stalks in fields where the adults and their children pulled it during the sizzling summers, after the corn ears were matured and the plants became brown streaks on a little green. To pull fodder we began at the top of the stalk and worked downward to the bottom. Using both hands, we snatched all the blades from one plant. Then we moved to the next plant, on our right, and stripped it clean also. When both hands were filled with the dying leaves, they were compressed into one hand while we grabbed yet another blade for "handing" the package, or tying it together with a unique sort of twist-n-tie that required the use of our thumbs. This packet, called a 'hand' was then thrust behind an ear of corn or pulled down over the broken-off plant top. As a fodder-puller we then moved on: pulling, 'handing,' hanging, pulling, 'handing,' hanging—all day long. "And never worrying about the blades cuttin' your hands 'cause they was tough enough to strike a match on," my good octogenarian friend, Mr. Ed, refreshed my memory recently.

"Many a time I remember pulling fodder all day long for fifty cents," Mr. Ed continued. "Big land owners'd hire a bunch to come in and we'd have a time racing to see who could pull the most fodder. Two, three days later, depending on the weather, we'd come back and get the dried fodder in. We'd grab up three of the dried 'hands' of fodder, snatch out one blade and tie the three together to make one 'bundle.' You'd go around them, twist it and make a loop, like looping under a belt; you could sure bet on it a'holding. And then we'd tote the bundles to the end of the rows. The wagon'd come along and pick them up, take 'em to the barns and stack them in the lofts. You had to be careful not to put it in too quick, 'fore it dried, or it'd go through a heat and then it wouldn't be good for the mules after it molded."

"I can remember hard times when folks'd borrow fodder from one another—borrow whatever yer neighbor could let you have, to last you through the winter, and on through the spring, too," Mr. Ed went on.

"Then when the pasture was gone, we'd feed the fodder to the mules. They got two bundles of fodder at night, along with their 15 ears of corn. If they were working they got eight, ten ears of corn—but no fodder—at dinnertime; if they weren't working, we just turned them out to graze. If the pasture was dead, that was their problem," added the oldster.

Now although Mr. Ed said, "Fodder wadn't no 'count, really nothing to it; top's got some strength in it—I'd rather have the tops two-to-one," this old farmer is kinda negative about fodder, but Daddy never felt that way. When my brother Bill and I questioned the good of us slaving in that hot corn patch, stinging like the nettle rash from those fuzzy corn blades, Daddy always said, "Having fodder'll sure beat eating snow."

Pulling fodder was something the entire family could do; my grandpap pulled past 80 and my Uncle Ferman remembers helping a neighbor by pulling fodder when he was tall enough to only reach the bottom two or three blades. He pulled, then passed to a taller boy who snatched the high ones and tied them together.

My uncle Claude thinks breaking the tops out

of his corn stalks, about the time the roast'n ears were finished, helped the corn to grow bigger and cure better long ago. He said that he used to break his tops and shock them up out in the fields.

Mr. Ed recently told how he and his family were "really uptown when it came to 'breaking the tops.'" His dad had some old homemade knives which were kept sharpened to use for clipping the corn tops (and stripping cane). He said they cut the tops just above the roast'n ears and treated it much the same way they did fodder: bundled it, let it dry, and then stored it in the loft.

"Pea vine hay was lots more advanced than fodder," according to Mr. Ed. He refers, however, to later years when "old speckled peas were broadcast in the fields. After you'd eat all you'd wanted and they'd got almost dried you came along and cut them with a mower. They dried a day, then you raked them in wind rows, dragged the rows to the baler and baled them in the little long bales." Now THAT was more advanced than fodder!

If any of you hard-hit farmers have to revert back to feeding pea vines like my Uncle Ferman, now in his 80s, also remembers doing, then he has a word of warning for you about this not-so-advanced, risky business.

"Once we 'uz cutting the pea vines from the field, with hoes, to dry for the stock and Aunt Harriet just *pulled up* a big pile and throwed 'em over the fence into th' lot. The next morning Ma's cow was laying there dead. All that nit'gen in them little knots on the roots killed 'er. Was the same thing that happened once when we tore down an old house out in the pasture. Our cow got in there where we'd stored some busted sacks of nit'rit sodie and et a bit; she just came wobblin' home. I yelled for Gertrude to mix eggs and coffee to dranch her with and ran across the holler to get Willie and Tillman to help but when I got back she was already dead. That nit'gen did it; just like on the pea vine roots. You gotta be careful with them pea vines."

My friend Gussie's got still another suggestion for stock owners on how to make it through the winter. Last fall I happened upon him watching his wife Ida shovel cotton seeds into the crib for feeding the cows during the coming cold. "They love 'em," he said, "feed's got so high we just started back feeding the seeds to the cows like we did 20, 30 years ago. There're a sight cheaper than anything else. Another good thing to feed 'em is to mix a lot of cotton seed hulls with just a handful of the cotton seed meal; it's real good fer 'em."

Like I said, times are hard again. If you young farmers 're gonna make it you may have to switch back to pea vine hay, corn tops, and borrowing fodder. I felt like it was coming when I saw my neighbor, Mr. Andrew, had sowed his field in Johnson grass.

Mama's Christmas Miracles

Old Man Depression seemed determined to squeeze Christmas right off Mama's calendar in 1933. The loss of two jobs by my Dad within the year had been financially disastrous for them. On Christmas Eve Mama went to the Five-and-Ten with her skimpy sewing earnings, their last hedge against poverty. While choosing a few small items for those dear she spied a little waif and his two tiny sisters. They were only wistful observers amid the happy shoppers. Drawn to the yearning children, Mama soon knew that their father, too, was out of work and their mother could sew. They left clutching with unbelief the gifts of shirt and dress fabric, china dolls, and spinning top. Their laughing, grateful eyes crystallized Mama's goals.

Then and there she resolved to make like-miracles happen not just at, but especially at Christmastime for the rest of her life.

Hard times passed for some: for us they hung on forever, giving Mama lots of practice with the miracle-making. Reduced to the red hilly soil of tenant farming we were left with little more than our faith in God and creativeness for Christmas joy. Many of our neighbors, in like situations, skipped the observance altogether. Not so our house.

Mama's Christmas dreams began taking shape 'ere summer ended. Extra vegetables brought just enough to order the plaid wool from the catalogue. It was masterfully transformed during fall school hours into a stylish overcoat to surprise her teenage daughter. The dolls which disappeared in late November were not seen again 'til Christmas morn. They then looked like new in fashions of the day, and some even had fresh parts like tummies, legs, or arms. Stuffed dolls and dogs were crafted for small boys. And, always, Mama made some extras for "the poor."

Lacking money for even trinkets from the store she helped each child to plan, then make, something for the others—and for their many friends and teachers, too. With nine busy sibling-elves it was tough finding private workshops in a four-room house. Thus it came to be that one year Mama supervised my completion of brother's stuffed squirrel in the distant cold corncrib.

When the fire on Christmas Eve was only

embers, the clean but ragged stockings were tacked to the mantel's shelf. When the last child had camouflaged their sleep Daddy slipped to the neighbor's for the fruit he'd bought in town that day. The Mason jars from out of the trunk yielded up their well-kept secrets of homemade fudge, caramels, and taffy—to be wrapped carefully around in waxed paper from a roll.

Then Mama laid out the miracles, or placed them in the socks, and went—exhausted but fulfilled—to her bed. Soon Dad gave answer to the first child's call. By 3 a.m. he made the fire. And seeing all the joy and wondrous love for everything she'd fashioned there, he lost the sadness that he'd felt because he was too poor to buy.

Always the Christmas meal—the rooster and the dressing, the yams, the homemade rolls, the cakes—were shared with others in our neighborhood who then were sick or old or destitute. The tree, with all its miracle of decorations made from popcorn strings and silvery ices cut from Dad's tobacco cans, mirrored the joy within our hearts and was the envy of our friends.

When Mama talks of Christmas now the twinkle in her eye belies her 80 years. It speaks instead of youth. And miracles. Of how she sews and shops all year and yet when dawns the 24th she'll think of yet another gift to make: a neighbor down the street who's lonely now or someone in the nursing home of whom she's heard. The little boy who lives nearby with handicap and oft seems shy and is left out—he'll sure be asked to join her cookie-baking time.

She frets not of the cost nor of the paltry little check on which she lives. Anticipation of the great-grand's eyes when the fur koala bear he gets is all the compensation that she seeks as now she sews with twisted pain-filled hands the last of beady eyes. And the undershirt wrapped up, the size 66 for that teasing son-in-law—that'll fix him good and light her face as well.

The falling stovepipe with soot left in its wake failed years ago to quench Mama's festive spirit on Christmas morn. If anything, the laughter from it all increased her joy. The mess and aggravation of 50 offsprings gathered in her tiny place on Christmas Eve now does the same. And when each their miracle has unwrapped and the last goodbye is said—she goes again to her bed—exhausted but fulfilled. And she drifts off planning for next year's Christmas Miracles and thinking of the good life we've had with *Pot Likker, Pulley Bones, and Pea Vine Hay.*

I'm Much Obliged . . .

To all those who worked and sacrificed that I might enter "Author" instead of "Housewife" on opinion polls:

My husband, Joe, who ate a million pot pies.

My publisher and editors, John and Deborah Seymour, who tolerated my free-flowing red pen on the final galleys.

My illustrator and sister, Trillie Brown, who bargained for "rough sketches" and got stuck with depicting the mites underneath the distant whippoorwill's wings.

My photographer, Justina Strong, who held the time exposure while I licked a little 'lasse candy.

And my designer, Sherry Price, who—after my mind-changes had worn her pencil to the nub—finished the cover in her own blood, anxious for an appropriate threshold through which you might enter to enjoy **Pot Likker, Pulley Bones, and Pea Vine Hay.**

Author and Her Mama . . .

(Photo by Justina Strong)

FAYE BROWN's humor has been whetted by:

- Fighting stinging worms on the back forty of a tenant farm with four brothers and four sisters.
- Bathing in Granny's lye soap.
- Thirty–one years of marriage to a man whose days begin with, "Faye, gettin' you another rabbit dog to train."
- Three children who set world verbal records: crying as babies, volunteering mom as kids, and phone rapping as teens.

Over the past three years Faye has learned "*there is* life after PTA." During that time her nostalgia and humorous satire column has become syndicated and she has been published in the following magazines: *Neighbors, Mid–South, Mature Living, The Blade, Country Woman, AREA, Rural Heritage, Small Farmer's Journal,* and *Tennessee Farm Bureau News.*

Additional Book Selections From SEVGO Press . . .

Papa's Legacy, the sequel to *Papa's Old Trunk*, is Eclectic, Alabama author Mary Kimbro Butler's moving story of a Deep South farm family's escapades, adventures, and struggles to survive the Great Depression, WWII, and the hectic aftermath years . . . helped by the legacy of a father who died too soon.

NO. SP-10 . . . . . $7.50 Pa*
$15.95 HC

Take A Whistler's Walk by Joyce C. Reed, Selma, Alabama wife, mother, author, artist, and real estate sales professional. This exciting story is ideal for those pre-teens and early teens who love adventure. Meribeth and Drusilla solve a riddle and discover the stolen family fortune in true Nancy Drew style.

NO. SP-09 . . . . $4.50 Pa
$15.95 HC

A Pear For The Teacher by Daisy Styles, retired university faculty member, mother, wife, and tireless church worker from Holt, Alabama. Her book gets a "Must Read" label for those families with an exceptional child from Pediatrician D. A. Reese. Mrs. Styles brings over 30 years of loving work with all types of exceptional children to the pages of her book.

NO. SP-02 . . . . . $7.95 Pa

Tales From The Sidewalk Benches by Jimmy Acton, a police officer with Livingston University. A published songwriter, poet, and raconteur par excellence, Jimmy spins yarns that keep the reader spellbound, almost believing you are sitting on the courthouse steps listening to the Old Timers.

NO. SP-04 . . . . . $7.50 Pa

Dangerous Innocence is a true story by Mobile's Cheryl Morgan which describes a secretary's flight and terror as the Mafia places a contract on her life when she overhears too much at her office. Assuming a new identity, the heroine of this story still looks over her shoulder when out in public.

NO. SP-11 . . . . . $7.50 Pa

CAMI And Other Familiar Friends by Della Dockery, a Hurley, Mississippi senior citizen and artist. A storybook to color, Della's book is also suitable for watercolors and is equally good for supervised or independent activity by the preschool child. Della became an author in her seventieth year.

NO. SP-03 . . . . . $2.95 Pa